Leo Cacioppo

W9-BNK-583

PROJECT 2002

JOHN CARROLL

BARNES
&NOBLE
BOOKS
NEW YORK

In easy steps is an imprint of Computer Step
Southfield Road . Southam
Warwickshire CV47 0FB . United Kingdom
www.ineasysteps.com

This edition published for Barnes & Noble Books, New York
FOR SALE IN THE USA ONLY
www.bn.com

Copyright © 2003 by Computer Step. All rights reserved. No part of
this book may be reproduced or transmitted in any form or by any
means, electronic or mechanical, including photocopying, recording,
or by any information storage or retrieval system, without prior
written permission from the publisher.

Notice of Liability
Every effort has been made to ensure that this book contains
accurate and current information. However, Computer Step and the
author shall not be liable for any loss or damage suffered by readers
as a result of any information contained herein.

Trademarks
Microsoft® and Windows® are registered trademarks of Microsoft
Corporation. All other trademarks are acknowledged as belonging to
their respective companies.

Printed and bound in the United Kingdom

ISBN 0-7607-4787-3

Contents

Consolidation   215

18

Advanced Topics   221

19

Index   233

The Basics

This chapter explains what Microsoft Project 2002 is and how it can help you to manage your project. It provides some background to projects and project management and then introduces the main features of Project 2002.

Covers

Chapter One

Introduction

Microsoft Project 2002 is a great project management tool. Managing projects can be a complex activity but, with the help of Project 2002, you can plan, schedule and control the progress of your project.

Why do you need to plan and control your project? Well, statistically, around 50% of business projects are not successful. If you don't plan and control your project, the chances are that it will be among that 50%!

This book covers Project 2002. If you have an earlier version of Microsoft Project some of the features may be unavailable or slightly different.

Whether your project is a simple, short-term one (such as arranging a company meeting) or a more complex project (like developing a new computer system), Project 2002 will let you stay in control.

Used as a planning tool, Project 2002 can produce some great-looking charts to help you plan your project. But Project can do a lot more besides:

- It can help you allocate and schedule work, tasks and activities.

- It can produce a critical path analysis to identify where you will need to track progress carefully.

- It can identify if you have too much work allocated to any one person.

- It can schedule facilities such as meeting rooms and overhead projectors for you.

- It can interface with your email system or Internet browser to allow you to keep your team in the picture.

- It can publish to the Web using HTML and export files to Excel so you can produce charts/graphs of your project's progress.

Additionally, with the addition of Project Server (a companion product) you can collaborate and share your project data across the organization via an Intranet or the Web.

How to Use This Book

Each topic in this book is intended to be freestanding in its own right and you can just pick the topics you are interested in. If, however, you want to use it in a more structured way, the following are some general guidelines if you are not sure exactly where to begin:

If You're New to Project Management

Start at the beginning and work right the way through to Chapter 14. Use our example project to build up experience and test things and try them out as you go. Then go back to Chapter 3 and begin again with your real project for the maximum benefit.

If You're New to Project 2002 (But Not to Project Management)

If you've used another project planning tool, then skim through Chapters 1 to 3 and start at Chapter 4 (the examples should illustrate any differences). If you've not used another project planning tool, then work through from Chapter 1 (but skim the topics on project management).

If You've Used a Previous Version of Microsoft Project

Read "What's New in Project 2002" (the next topic) and skim the remainder of this chapter and Chapter 2, then work through from Chapter 4 looking out for the new features. In particular, read the chapter on Project Server as this is a completely new companion product to Project 2002 (replacing Project Central which first shipped with Project 2000).

The Exercises

The exercises throughout this book build up a project plan step by step.

 If you use July 1, 2003 as the start date for your exercise project your results should be exactly the same as the illustrations in this book.

The later topics build on the project and assume that you have saved it at the end of the previous topic. But don't worry if you have skipped any topics or chapters: you should be able to see from the screen shots what's happening and be able to recreate them. If not, just go back to the previous topic and follow the steps there.

What's New in Project 2002?

New Editions and Options

There are a number of quite significant enhancements and changes in Project 2002, compared to earlier versions. To start with there are now two editions – Project Standard 2002 and Project Professional 2002 – plus two new server options: Project Server 2002 and Project Server 2002 Client Access Licenses (CALs).

Project Standard

Microsoft Project Standard 2002 is the basic product, which includes all the essential project management features. It is the latest version and provides all the features that were in earlier versions of Project such as Project 2000 and Project 98. These include task scheduling, resource management, progress tracking, reporting, customization and flexibility. In addition it provides team collaboration (introduced with Project 2000) when used with Project Server 2002.

"Enterprise" is the term Microsoft uses to refer to larger businesses.

Project Professional

Microsoft Project Professional 2002 is aimed at the enterprise. It is scalable across multiple departments and groups and, in addition to the features of Project Standard, it provides the capability to standardize and customize the way Project is used across an organization.

Project Server

Microsoft Project Server 2002 replaces Project Central (which was first shipped with Project 2000). It provides the platform for collaboration and enterprise project management. It can be accessed from Project Standard, Project Professional or using a standard Web browser such as Microsoft Internet Explorer with Client Access Licenses (CALs).

Project Server CALs

Microsoft Project Server CALs 2002 provides Client Access Licenses to enable project team members and other stakeholders to access centrally stored project information using a Web browser (Microsoft recommend Internet Explorer 5.5 or later). This means that team members do not need to have Project 2002 installed to access project information.

New and Improved Features

In addition to the new editions and options, a number of new and improved features have also been introduced:

Project Guide

You can turn the Project Guide off when you no longer need it!

This new feature provides step by step, wizard-like instructions and controls in the left-hand pane to help you create a new project, manage tasks and resources, specify and change working time, track progress and report project information.

Smart Tags

These give you feedback and advice on alternative actions as you delete task or resource names, change resource assignments, start and finish dates, work, units or duration.

Collaboration Menu

Gives access to Project Server pages and features directly from within Project.

Assign Resources

In the Assign Resources dialog box you can now search and filter for appropriate resources and see graphs of availability.

Track Actuals

You can use the status date to view progress more efficiently and reduce the number of steps required when entering actuals, especially percent completed or percent work completed.

Rescheduling Uncompleted Work

Any constraints remain as originally set when you reschedule uncompleted work. You can also choose any reschedule date that you like.

Multiple Baselines

You can now set as many as eleven baselines on a project rather than just one.

Baseline Data Rollup

You can control how baseline data is rolled up into summary tasks.

Earned Value Improvements

Additions to the Earned Value data include Schedule Performance Index (SPI), To Completion Performance Index (TCPI), Cost

Performance Index (CPI), Cost Variance Percent (CVP) and Schedule Variance Percent (SVP). You can also choose from the eleven baselines to calculate Earned Value data.

Network Diagram View
You can now group tasks and display graphical indicators in the Network Diagram view.

Usage Views
You can now group assignments and roll up grouped timephazed information in Usage views. You can also include totals when printing Usage views.

Timescales
You can now display three timescales in the Gantt Chart and other views instead of just two.

Microsoft Excel Integration
It is now easy to import data from and export data to Microsoft Excel as well as other supported file types.

Excel Task List Template
You can use the new Excel Task List Template to start a task list and then import it into Project 2002 without mapping any fields.

Microsoft Outlook Integration
You can also create a task list in Microsoft Outlook and import it into Project 2002.

Collaborative Management
There are a number of new features to help you manage a collaborative project using Project Web Access:

- Simplified Timesheet: to allow the project team to report their time in a standard way.

- Manager Transactions: allows you to review, filter and group summarized updates and task requests.

- Multiple Managers: allows more than one project manager to track tasks and resources in the same project.

- Task Lists: create and manage simple task lists on Project Server and open them in Project 2002.

- Resource Comments: maintain a history of resource comments compiled from task notes.

Team Member Collaboration

Using Microsoft Project Web Access, team members can use the instructions and controls in the left-hand pane to assist them with managing task lists, delegating tasks, reporting and viewing project information.

They can manage notification and reminders through the Access Transaction page. They can save a view and change indicators will appear when the data in a field has changed since the last update. When working on more than one project, they can send separate task updates for each project.

They can also update Project Server views and status reports from Microsoft Outlook.

Manage Documents and Issues

You can access the Document Library, enter Issues, track progress and create related reports through Project Web Access.

Administering collaborative projects

New views, functionality, roles and permissions have been created to make the administration of Project Server more flexible.

Customization

ActiveX controls for Project 2002 Server provide improved programmable interfaces and more options for extending and customizing Microsoft Project Web Access.

OLE DB Provider has been enhanced with timephazed data, additional tables and extended properties for data access pages.

XML format is now available as a file format for importing, exporting and saving files.

Installing Project 2002

Although 105MB of free space is the requirement for the typical installation, you will need more space if you wish to install some of the options under the custom installation. Try to start with 200MB or more of free space. The Setup program will warn you if you do not have enough room.

Installing Microsoft Project version 2002 is done by running the program SETUP.EXE. This will usually run automatically when the CD is inserted into the drive.

Before running Setup, make sure you have a suitable system. You need a PC with the following:

- Pentium III or higher processor with Windows 98/NT 4.0 with service pack 6 or later.

- At least 56MB of RAM (memory) on Windows 98/98 SE, 64MB on Windows Me or NT, 96MB on Windows 2000 and 160MB on Windows XP.

- 105MB of free disk space for a typical installation (55MB if you have Office XP installed) or up to 310MB for a full installation without Office XP installed.

- CD-ROM drive.

- SuperVGA or higher resolution monitor.

The first thing that Setup does is ask for the Product Key which is on a sticker on the back of the CD case:

When installing large programs, it is easy to use almost all the space on your hard disk. Unfortunately, Windows needs free space for temporary files. You also need to allow space for your documents. It is best to keep 1GB or more free at all times.

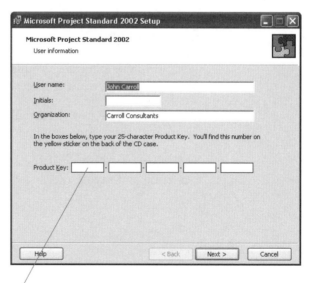

Enter the Product Key (there is no need to tab between boxes).

Next, Setup will ask you what type of install you require:

2 Select Install Now
for the standard
install or choose
Complete or
Custom as
required. Then
click Next.

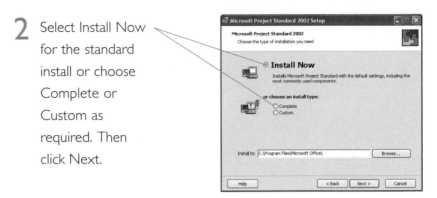

Microsoft Project tells you it is ready to begin installation.

3 Click Install to
begin installation.

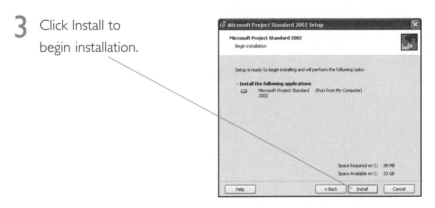

Project 2002 will then continue and complete the installation.

4 Click OK to complete
the installation.

The first time you open Project 2002 a Planning Wizard will appear
asking if you want to copy your global settings from the previous
version of Microsoft Project. This will import any changes you
have made to customize Project 2000 or Project 98. It will not be
able to import any changes to earlier versions.

Activating Project 2002

Once you have installed Microsoft Project 2002 you will need to activate it. It will allow you to use it up to 50 times before activation but it is better to get it over with as soon as possible.

The easiest way to activate the product is by Internet if you have a connection, otherwise you will need to activate it by telephone.

> Select the appropriate radio button and click Next.

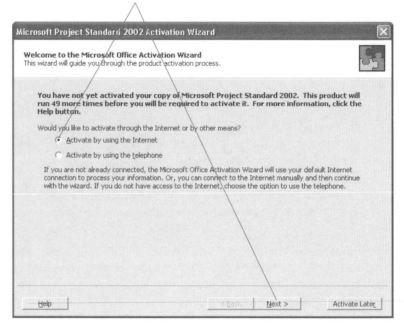

If you are activating by telephone Project will display the steps you should carry out and the telephone number you should call. It is a good idea to print this information so you have a record of it.

If you are activating over the Internet, the Activation Wizard will display a welcome screen with a privacy statement on the conditions of use of the information you provide.

2 If you are happy with the conditions click the Next button to continue with activation.

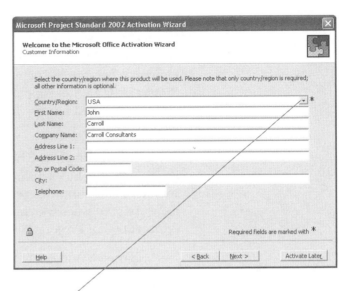

3 Select the Country or Region from the drop-down list, enter any other information you like and click Next to continue.

You can get help or cancel activation at any time using the Help and Activate Later buttons.

4 Enter your email address if you wish to be kept up-to-date with product updates and other information. Click Submit.

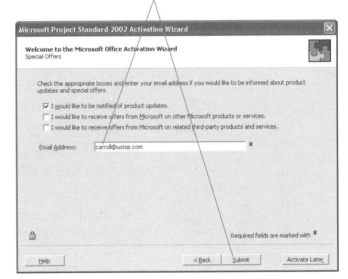

Project should now be activated and you are ready to go.

Migration from Previous Versions

While Project 2002 provides some significant enhancements over Project 2000, Microsoft have introduced backward compatibility with Project 2000 and to a more limited extent with Project 98. However, because the new and enhanced features introduced in Project 2002 are not supported in earlier versions, there could be some unexpected results. The issues are discussed in the following sections:

Scheduling Engine Changes

Project 2002 includes refinements to the scheduling engine which are intended to improve performance and precision. However, there are two issues which may affect project plans created in Project 2000 or Project 98:

1. Earned Value Analysis: the value of Estimate at Completion (EAC) is now calculated to take account of the Cost Performance Index (CPI).

2. Tracking: when editing %Complete, %Work Complete, Actual Work or Actual Duration, Project 2002 moves forward earlier remaining work to start at the status date and moves back later completed work to finish at the status date.

The following additional issues may affect project plans created in Project 98:

3. Task Scheduling: it is possible for schedule dates to change the first time a project is opened in Project 2002. The schedule should therefore be checked carefully after opening it for the first time in Project 2002.

4. Task Criticality: due to improvements in calculating the critical path, some tasks may shift on or off the critical path when an existing plan is opened in Project 2002.

5. Master Project Critical Path: a new feature allows Project 2002 to calculate a critical path for a master project across all sub-projects. To treat sub-projects the same way as in Project 98, clear Inserted projects are calculated like summary tasks in the Calculation Options dialog box.

Backward compatibility introduces the ability to open Project 2002 files in earlier versions of Project.

Backward Compatibility

While Project 2002 provides excellent backward compatibility with Project 2000 (and to a lesser extent Project 98). This will obviously depend on how much use is made of new features that are not supported in the earlier versions.

Project 2000

The file formats used by Project 2002 and Project 2000 are compatible and no information will be lost when a file created in Project 2002 is opened and saved in Project 2000. However, if the Save As command is used in Project 2000, the 2002 data will be lost. Other features that may be affected are:

1. Baselines: as Project 2000 only supports one baseline, any additional baselines will not be shown.

2. Earned Value: Project 2000 does not support the additional fields in Project 2002 so Earned Value calculations may be different.

3. Constraints: Project 2000 may not preserve task constraints when a project is updated and rescheduled.

Project 98

In addition to the issues listed above, the following features may also be affected in Project 98:

4. When a project is to be saved in Project 98 format, it must be saved in this format before a baseline is set or the timephazed baseline data will be lost.

5. Calendars: if five-shift calendars are used in Project 2002 they will be converted to three-shift calendars in Project 98.

6. Deadline Dates: Project 98 does not support deadline dates.

7. Estimated Duration: any estimated duration will be lost.

8. Formatting: any formatting that exceeded the capabilities of Project 98 will be lost.

9. Material Resources: Project 98 does not support Material Resources. These will be converted to Work Resources and material data lost when the project is saved in Project 98.

The Gantt Chart

The first thing you see when you open or create a new project is the Gantt Chart.

It is the default view, and with good reason. The Gantt Chart is probably the most widely used and most useful project management tool.

They say that every picture is worth a thousand words – this is the key picture in your project:

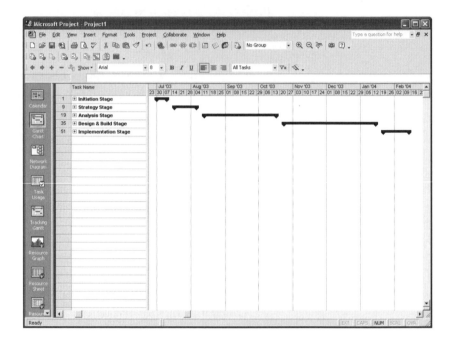

At the summary level (as shown above) you can view the whole project on one screen or on one sheet of paper. The Gantt Chart represents the most frequently used way of representing a project graphically and is particularly useful for senior management in its rolled-up summary form.

The Gantt Chart view is more than just a view, though. It also allows you to plan and control your project by inserting and editing project tasks, setting and changing project milestones and even allocating and controlling project resources.

Tasks and Milestones

At the detailed level in Gantt Chart view, you can view the individual Tasks and Project Milestones:

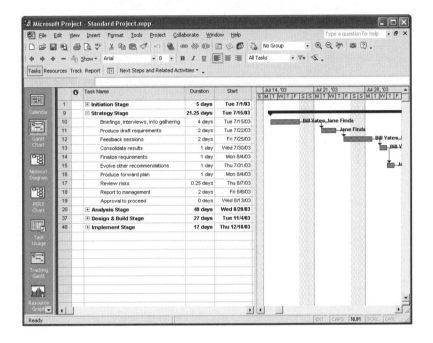

In Gantt Chart view you can:

- Expand or close up the list of tasks by clicking on the "+" or "–" beside any summary task or using the buttons on the Formatting Toolbar.

- See and edit the scheduled start date, duration and finish date for individual tasks.

- See and edit the linkages and dependencies between tasks.

- Set and change your project milestones.

- See who is allocated to each task and, if necessary, allocate more resources or change the allocation.

Resource Usage

Resources are the people and facilities that you will use on your project. You can track resource usage through both the Task Usage and Resource Usage views.

The Task Usage view allows you to see who and what is being used on each task:

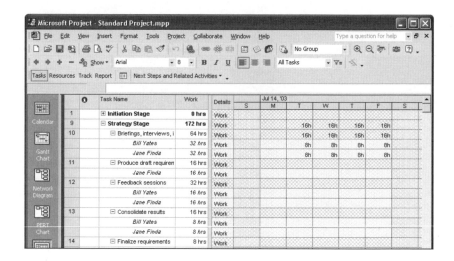

The Resource Usage view lets you see what each person is doing:

Resource Usage view enables you to monitor work assignments, identify potential problems due to overload and generally stay in firm control of your project.

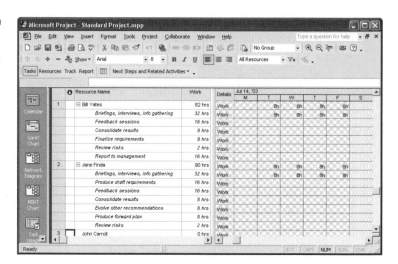

View Bar

While the Gantt Chart view is the default (and probably the most useful) view in Project 2002, there are another 25 predefined views. These can be selected through the View Bar.

HOT TIP *Although there are already 26 views in Project 2002, you can still create extra custom views of your own.*

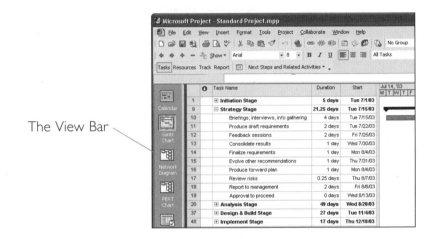

The View Bar

The View Bar can be used to switch back and forth between views. These are the views and their icons:

HOT TIP *The View Bar can be hidden to give you more room for your chart by clicking View> View Bar on the Menu Bar. To bring it back just click View> View Bar again (View Bar in the drop-down menu is checked).*

Calendar:	tasks and their duration.
Gantt Chart:	the default view of tasks/time.
Network Diagram:	a chart of tasks showing their links and dependencies.
Task Usage:	tasks and who is allocated.
Tracking Gantt:	shows actual against scheduled.
Resource Graph:	resource usage or cost over time.
Resource Sheet:	shows details of each resource.
Resource Usage:	shows a list of task assignments by resource.
More Views:	gives all 26 available views.

Toolbars

The Standard and Formatting Toolbars contain the standard Microsoft Office buttons together with a number of Project 2002 specific ones:

The buttons are:

This table omits those icons which are more or less standard to Windows programs (e.g. Bold and Italic).
(You can always find out what any button does by pausing the mouse pointer over it.)

Standard

 New Project

Open

Save

Print

Print Preview

Spell Check

Cut

Copy

Paste

Format Painter

Undo

Insert Hyperlink

Link Tasks

Unlink Tasks

Split Task

Information

Toolbar Options

 Notes

Assign Resources

Zoom In

Zoom Out

Go to selected task

Chart snapshot

Help

Formatting

Outdent

Indent

Show Subtasks

Hide Subtasks

Show options

Autofilter

Chart Wizard

If you don't see all of these buttons, you can use Toolbar Options to show others.

How to Get Help

There are several ways of getting help in Project 2002.

From the Menu Bar:

1 Select Help>Contents and Index.

2 Select the Contents Tab for a full list of contents, Answer Wizard to type a question or the Index Tab for a searchable Index.

Use the F1 key or click Help on the Button bar to open the Office Assistant.

To find out what something is, use Shift+F1 then point and click at the item you want to know about.

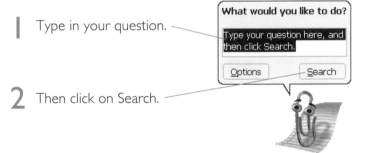

1 Type in your question.

2 Then click on Search.

You can even get Help from the Web using Help>Office on the Web from the Menu Bar:

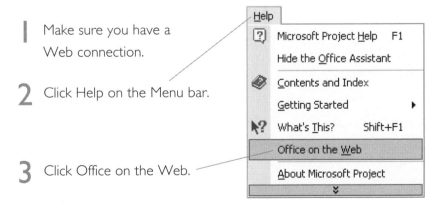

1 Make sure you have a Web connection.

2 Click Help on the Menu bar.

3 Click Office on the Web.

Getting Started

For a bit more information about the concepts of project management and an overview of the capabilities of Project 2002, you can get a Project Map, take a Tutorial or review What's New:

1 Select Help from the Menu bar.

2 Select Getting Started.

3 Select Project Map, Tutorial or What's New.

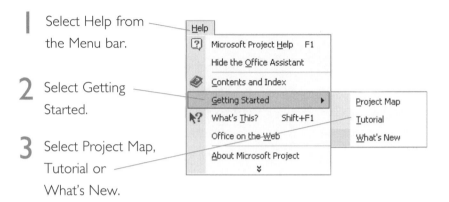

If you select Tutorial, the Tutorial will open at Microsoft Project: The Basics. Use the topics and slide controls to navigate through the Tutorial.

It is worthwhile taking a quick look at these features, particularly if you are new to project management.

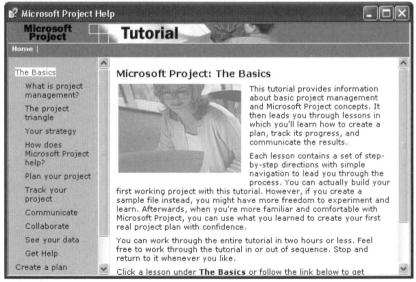

Project Map will give you a Web-style guide through the steps involved in creating a new project in Project 2002.

Project Guide

Project Guide is a new feature introduced in Project 2002. This chapter gives an introduction to it and explains the basic components and how they function.

Covers

Chapter Two

Project Guide

Microsoft has responded to suggestions that earlier versions of Microsoft Project were viewed by some users as complex, by introducing the Project Guide with Project 2002. This is intended to make the product easier to use for beginners and those users who do not have a full knowledge of the project management domain. It consists of three main components:

You can turn the Project Guide off when you no longer need it.

1. The toolbar displays top-level navigation buttons called the goal areas (Tasks, Resources, Track and Report) along with Show/Hide Project Guide and Next Steps buttons.

2. The side pane is used for navigation within each of the goal areas. In the illustration below the suggested activities for the Tasks goal area are displayed.

3. The main view area displays the conventional Project view.

| The Project Guide toolbar.

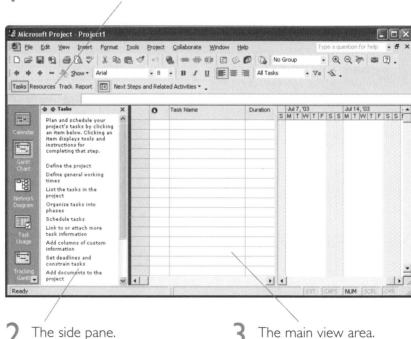

2 The side pane.   3 The main view area.

Goal Areas

The four standard goal areas are Tasks, Resources, Track and Report. Selecting each of them brings up an appropriate list of activities in the side pane.

Tasks

The Tasks goal area will help you to set your project up initially and list the work to be done. It contains activities to: set the start date and file name; set up the project calendars; enter the tasks that will make up the project; structure the tasks into stages or phases; schedule the tasks by adding dependencies; attach notes or hypertext links; add custom information; set deadlines and constraints on tasks; and (if you have access to Project Server) add documents to the project and publish information to the Web.

Resources

The Resources goal area allows you to define the people and material resources that will be used to carry out the project. It contains activities to: define the resources; set up calendars for them; assign them to tasks; add notes and hypertext links; add custom information; and (if you have access to Project Server) publish project information to the Web.

Track

Once your project is under way the Track goal area will help you to update the project with progress achieved. It contains activities to: set a baseline; update tasks with progress information; check the progress of the project; make changes to tasks and resources; and (if you have access to Project Server) track issues, request status reports and publish project information to the Web.

Report

While the Goal areas can be used to carry out all these activities, they can additionally be carried out directly in Project 2002.

In addition to tracking progress you will also want to view and report on it and support is provided under the Report goal area. It contains activities to: produce a report; change the report content or format; change the Gantt Chart; compare progress to the baseline; or set the critical path and view assignments/project costs.

The next few topics will step through the process of using goal areas to perform some basic project activities.

Task Goal Area

1 Project Guide should open each time you start a new project. If not, click on the Show/Hide Project Guide button and Project Guide will open.

2 Click on the Tasks button.

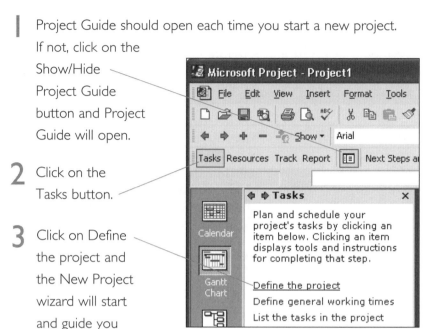

3 Click on Define the project and the New Project wizard will start and guide you through the process.

4 Select the date you want your project to start using the drop-down calendar (or type the date). Then click on Save and go to Step 2.

5 In Step 2 of 4 select No to collaborate (we deal with it later) and go on to Step 3.

We deal with defining working time later and will list the tasks in the topic on the facing page.

6 In Step 3 of 4 enter the file name "Project Guide" for your project and save it when asked.

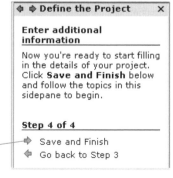

7 Finally in Step 4 of 4 click Save and Finish.

Listing the Tasks

We will deal with tasks in much more detail in later topics.

The key activity in the Tasks goal area is listing the tasks. These are the basic building blocks of the project.

1 Open the Project Guide, Select Tasks and click on List the tasks in the project.

The side pane now tells you how to enter task/duration details (see below).

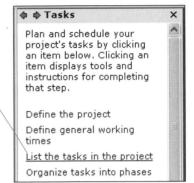

2 Enter some task names and durations.

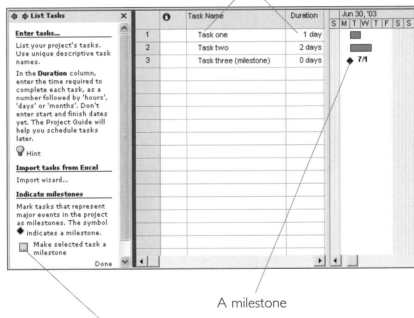

A milestone

We will also deal with milestones in more detail in a later topic.

3 Click on Make selected task a milestone to create a milestone.

4 Click on Done at the bottom of the side pane to finish creating tasks and milestones.

Resources

Once you have put in the tasks for your project you will need to enter details of the resources: people that will do the work and material that will be used. The Resources goal area lists some of the appropriate activities.

1 Open Project Guide and select Resources.

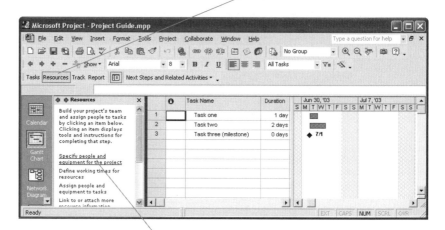

2 Click on Specify people and equipment for the project and you will be given the options of selecting people from a company address book, directory or server or entering them manually.

We will be looking at resources in much more detail in later topics.

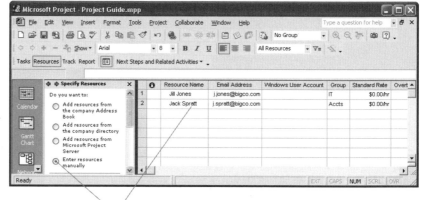

3 Select Enter resources manually and type in the details. When you have finished click Done at the bottom of the side pane.

Track

Once you have put in the tasks and resources for your project you will need to start tracking progress. The Track goal area lists some of the appropriate activities.

1 Open Project Guide and select Track.

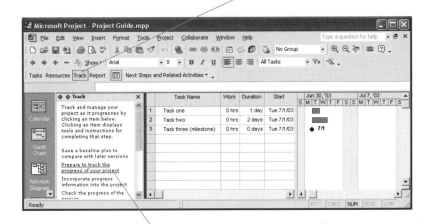

2 Select Prepare to track the progress of your project. You will be asked if you want your team to report through Project Server. Select No for manual report and updates and click Save and go to Step 2.

3 Select tracking method Always track by entering percentage of work complete and click Save and finish.

We will look at tracking progress in more detail in later topics.

4 Select Incorporate progress and begin entering progress.

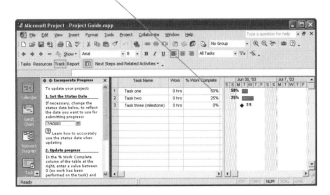

Reports

Once you have put in the tasks and resources and started tracking progress you will need to analyze and report on it. The Report goal area lists some of the appropriate activities.

1 Open Project Guide and select Report.

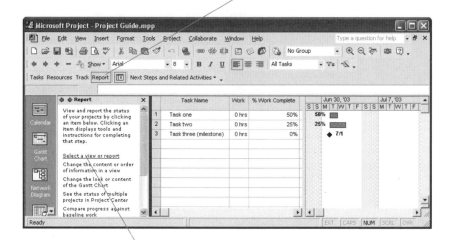

2 Click Select a view or report then select Print a project report. Click Display reports and finally the Reports dialog box opens.

3 Select Current activities, Tasks in progress and Unstarted tasks. The report will be produced – see below:

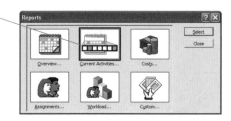

Reports are dealt with in much more detail in later topics.

Unstarted Tasks as of Mon 4/28/03
Project Guide

ID	Ö	Task Name	Duration	Start	Finish	Predecessors
1		Task one	1 day	Tue 7/1/03	Tue 7/1/03	
2		Task two	2 days	Tue 7/1/03	Wed 7/2/03	
3		Task three (milestone)	0 days	Tue 7/1/03	Tue 7/1/03	

If there is no data available try selecting Tasks in progress.

Managing Your Project

This chapter introduces a structured approach to managing a project and explores the ways in which Project 2002 can help you manage your project.

Covers

Chapter Three

A 4-Step Approach

Project management is the management of change.

In order to manage change and therefore manage your project, you need to carry out a number of steps or tasks. But rather than just jumping straight in and defining these steps or tasks, it is a good idea to take a more structured approach to a project.

These four steps will give you just that:

Experienced project managers may feel this is a simplistic approach. It is, but be patient as we will build on it in later sections.

1 Start by identifying what you are trying to achieve: define your project aims, goals or objectives. Where you want to get to...

2 Then plan how you will get there: once you have identified your project objectives, you can begin to map out what you are going to do to achieve them.

3 Carry it out: do it or manage it.

4 Hand it over: once the project is completed you have finished your job.

An awful lot of projects seem to start at Step 3! It's what's known as the "Just Do It" school of management. But even if you start your project at Step 2, what's the use of a plan if you don't know where you are going? So start by clearly identifying your goals.

Interestingly, the difficult step for some project managers is the last one. They find it difficult to let go.

The project manager's job is to implement change. Once that change has been implemented their role as a project manager is completed. The new, changed state becomes a production process and that requires production (rather than project) management.

In the remainder of this chapter we will expand on each of these four steps and look at what is involved, starting with Step 1, defining your objectives.

Step 1 – Define Your Objectives

The first step in any project is to define your objectives. You need to define your objectives in order to be able to:

- Make sure you have identified the right target.

- Focus the other members of the project team on what the project is about.

- Create team commitment to, and agreement about, the project objectives.

- Ensure that you involve all interested parties in achieving a successful project outcome.

When you set out to define your objectives there is a useful acronym to remember: SMART. Objectives need to be: Strategic; Measurable; Agreed; Realistic; and Timed.

Strategic	your objectives must address some strategic business purpose or need. If they do not, does the project really matter to the business and, if not, why carry it out?
Measurable	if you can't measure project achievement, how will you know if you've achieved anything?
Agreed	if the rest of the business and the rest of the project team have not agreed with the objectives, there will be no commitment to them.
Realistic	if the objectives are not realistic, the project team will soon realize that and lose any commitment to the project.
Timed	if there is no pressure to complete the project it will never get completed.

When you define your objectives, make sure that they are SMART.

Note: some people use a different set of words for the SMART acronym (e.g. Specific, Measurable, Assignable or Achievable, Realistic and Time-related). It doesn't matter which words you use as long as they achieve a similar effect.

So think about your project objectives now. Have you defined them adequately and are they SMART?

Keep It Simple

Another useful acronym to remember when thinking about your project objectives is KISS. It stands for: Keep It Short and Simple.

Your objectives should not only be SMART, they also need to be brief and simple to understand. If not, someone out there will misunderstand them!

If you don't keep it simple, below is a little reminder of what can go wrong:

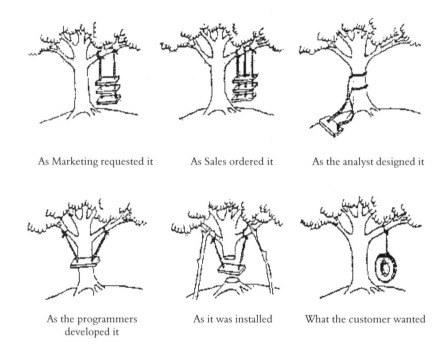

As Marketing requested it   As Sales ordered it   As the analyst designed it

As the programmers   As it was installed   What the customer wanted
developed it

So spend some more time making sure that your project objectives are stated simply. Make sure you know what you want to achieve then make sure other people are clear about your goals. The best way to do that is to show your objectives to other people and ask for their feedback.

An example: "In order to free up cash for business expansion, the project aims to achieve a reduction in stock-holding of 20% by the end of the financial year." That is a simple objective that is also SMART (if it is realistic and agreed).

Starting a Project

Start Project 2002 by clicking on Start>Programs>Project 2002. Project 2002 opens in Gantt Chart view with a blank project file and you can begin entering information about your project.

The Project Information dialog box may open automatically when you create a new project. This can be turned on or off from the Tools>Options>General tab.

1 Click Project>Project Information on the Menu Bar. The Project Information dialog box opens.

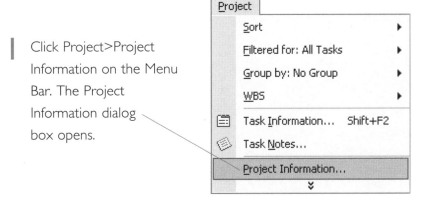

2 By default, the Start date will be the current date. If you want to change it, click the control beside the date box to open a calendar and select the date.

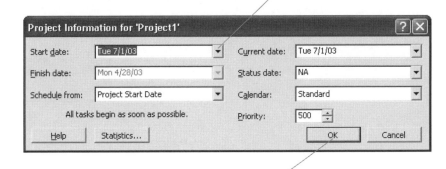

3 When you're happy with your start date, click the OK button.

Scheduling backwards from a finish date is much more difficult and is best avoided until you have some experience of forward scheduling.

By default, the project is scheduled forward from the Start date. You can also schedule backwards from a finish date by selecting Schedule from: Project Finish Date and entering your finish date.

Entering Summary Information

Once you've opened your project and set the start date you can begin to enter your objectives and other summary information in Project Properties.

1 Click File>Properties on the Menu Bar and the Project Properties dialog box opens. Select the Summary tab if not already selected.

2 Type the Title, Subject, your name and your Company name (if relevant).

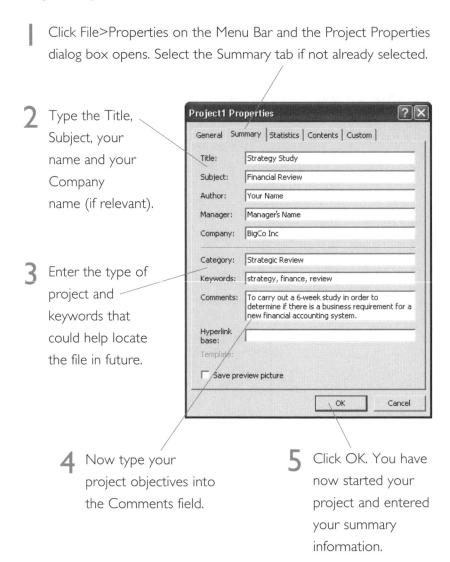

3 Enter the type of project and keywords that could help locate the file in future.

4 Now type your project objectives into the Comments field.

5 Click OK. You have now started your project and entered your summary information.

Now you have entered the summary information you can move on to "Step 2 – Develop Your Plan".

Step 2 – Develop Your Plan

Having defined your project objectives, the next step is to plan how you will achieve them, how you will get there, by developing your project plan.

Before we start building the plan we need to look at some of the key things that make up a project plan. These are:

- Tasks

- Deliverables

- Milestones

- Resources

Tasks

Tasks are the basic building blocks of the project. In order to carry out a project you will need to carry out a sequence of individual but interrelated tasks.

Deliverables

Deliverables not only allow you to measure completion, they also allow you to carry out quality assurance.

Deliverables (sometimes referred to as the Products of a project) are the things that the project will produce along the way. Typically, they consist of reports, requirements specifications, design documents and acceptance certificates as well as the final product (whatever it is).

Milestones

Milestones are the points during the project when you can accurately measure your progress. They will typically be major events like agreement of requirements, approval to proceed or final acceptance.

Resources

Resources are the people and other things you will use on the project to carry out the tasks and produce the deliverables.

Your project plan will consist of the *Tasks* needed to produce the *Deliverables* and complete the project, together with the *Resources* you will use to perform them and the *Milestones* you will use to measure your progress.

We will now look at each of these in a bit more detail.

Key Tasks and Deliverables

Any project consists of a number of tasks which need to be completed. It may consist of very few tasks or a very large number. Some tasks will be short tasks and others will take longer to complete. Some will be critical to the success of the project, while others may be less important.

The first step in producing your project plan is to begin listing the key tasks – the important ones, the ones that are critical to the success of the project. These will typically be related to a key deliverable. For example, if you were building a house, there would be a "design" task which would have the "house plans" as its deliverable.

If your project was to carry out a strategy study, the key tasks and deliverables would be something like:

Don't start typing in these tasks yet. We will do that in the next chapter.

Key Tasks	Deliverables
Plan the study	Project Plan
Information gathering	Interview Notes
Produce draft requirements	Draft Requirements
Hold feedback sessions	Final Requirements
Develop recommendations	Recommendations
Perform risk analysis	Risk Log
Produce implementation plan	Implementation Plan
Report to management	Final Report

While you may well have many other tasks to carry out during your project and may have other deliverables you need to produce, these should represent the major ones.

If you are not sure about whether a task is a key task or not, play safe and include it. It is easy to remove something later if it is not required but missing something key could be fatal.

Project Milestones

Project milestones are the events that mark the completion of a major task or group of tasks in a project.

Typical milestones would be the decision to proceed, selection of a supplier, acceptance of a major piece of work and, of course, completion of the project. Milestones often mark the acceptance of a key deliverable.

A milestone normally has a zero duration. In other words, it marks a single point in time when something happens.

Although a milestone will usually have zero duration, it is possible to set a milestone with a duration (we deal with this in a later topic).

Once you have identified the key tasks and their deliverables in your project, you need to identify the major milestones. For a short project (such as our strategy study) there may be only one milestone – completion of the project.

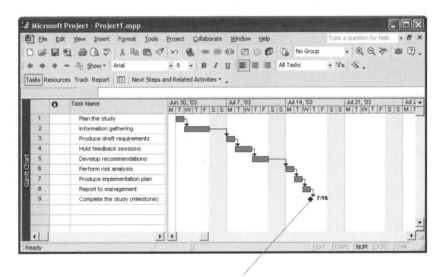

Project milestone

For a longer project there will be more, typically somewhere between three and eight milestones.

Now take another look at your project key tasks and identify what you think your project milestones are or should be.

We will start to enter these tasks/milestones in the next chapter.

Resources

The key resources on most projects are people: the project manager (you) and anyone else you are going to use to do any work on the project.

1   Click on Resource Sheet in the View Bar (it is near the base so you may need to scroll down). The Resource Sheet view opens:

You can also open Resource Sheet view by clicking View> Resource Sheet on the Menu Bar.

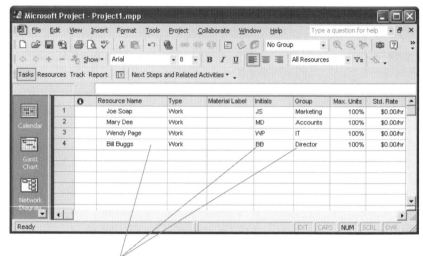

2   Type in the names, initials and group for all the people who will be involved on your project. Leave the defaults in the other fields for now.

3   Then identify any other resources or facilities that your project will need and type them in after the people. Change their Type to Material:

	❶	Resource Name	Type	Material Label	Initials	Group	Max. Units
1		Joe Soap	Work		JS	Marketing	100%
2		Mary Dee	Work		MD	Accounts	100%
3		Wendy Page	Work		WP	IT	100%
4		Bill Buggs	Work		BB	Director	100%
5		Project Room	Material	Room		Facilities	
6		Personal Computer	Material	PC		Facilities	

Don't worry about the other columns in the Resource Sheet; we will be dealing with them later.

The Full Works

While the Gantt Chart produced by Project 2002 presents a good visual representation of the project plan, you may need to produce a more formal project document at the end of the planning exercise. This will be likely if it is a larger project or you require some sort of formal authority to proceed.

Project Plan

The following suggested content is based on a formal project plan and should be entered using your usual word processing software. It should have the following sections:

One of the greatest problems in project management is not getting the key people or other resources you need when you need them.

1. Background: why the project is taking place.

2. The objectives of the project: what it aims to achieve.

3. Any prerequisites: things that must be available for the project to begin or continue.

4. External dependencies: any outside agencies that may be involved as suppliers, partners or clients.

5. Planning assumptions: anything that could have an impact on the project.

6. Project Gantt Chart: the summary level chart showing the main project stages.

7. Key deliverables: the tangible things that the project will produce or deliver.

8. Budget: the finance required to carry out the project in terms of real cost and nominal people cost (if relevant).

9. Resource requirements: the key people and any other resources that the project will need to be successful. This should include the percentage of time they have to have available for the project.

Even if you are not carrying out the project for anyone else, it's still a good idea to produce an Outline Plan.

This document forms the basis for agreement with your client, project sponsor, management, etc., and they will need to approve it for the project to continue. It is also good to show the project team what the project is about, and give them a chance to question and understand it. Don't forget the "A" in SMART stands for Agreed.

Step 3 – Carry It Out

One of the greatest mistakes made on projects is to jump straight in and get started. If you've skipped steps 1 and 2, go back and do them!

If you've been through Step 1 (Define Your Objectives) and Step 2 (Develop Your Plan), then you know where you're going and you have a plan for how you're going to get there. You will also have obtained any business approval you need to continue. You can now start carrying the project out.

There is often business pressure to skip these initial steps, particularly on smaller projects. It might sound good sense to just get stuck straight in and not waste time but it should be resisted. Carrying out a project without having clearly defined objectives and a proper plan is like building a new type of bridge from A to B, without knowing exactly where A is, and with the sure certainty that B will have moved by the time you get there.

Put simply, carrying out the project consists of allocating the necessary resources to the required tasks, tracking progress of the tasks until they are completed and measuring progress against your project milestones.

If only life were that simple the world would be a lovely place, but along comes Mr. Murphy:

Murphy's Law seems to apply doubly to IT projects.

Murphy's 1st Law

Whatever *can* go wrong,

will go wrong

So you also need to expect and to deal with problems. If you don't your project could rapidly get knocked off course. If you do, you can also benefit from the corollary to Murphy's First Law: "If you plan on it going wrong, it won't".

Saving Your Project

The chances are that, sooner or later, everyone who works with a computer will lose a large amount of work through a power cut or some other problem outside their control. I have even heard of some people (not me, of course) who caused the problem themselves!

So whenever you are working on a computer, save your work regularly. Project 2002 is no exception to this rule. By saving your work regularly you can try things out and always be able to get back to where you were. So save your project (and your sanity) by saving your work before (if you haven't already done so) and after making any major changes.

You can also click File>Save on the Menu Bar.

1 To save your file (replacing the previous version) simply click the Save button 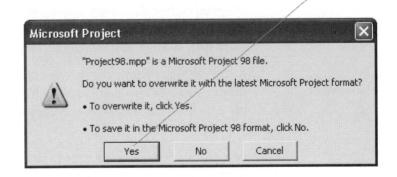 on the Toolbar.

2 If you want to preserve the previous version of the project click File>Save As from the Menu Bar. Enter the directory where you want to save the file and new file name and click Save.

3 If you save a project that was originally created in Project 98 you will get a dialog box asking if you want to save it in Project 98 format (click No) or Project 2002 format (click Yes):

Project 2002 also contains an AutoSave feature. In the Toolbar, go to Tools> Options>Save>Auto Save.

Microsoft Project

"Project98.mpp" is a Microsoft Project 98 file.

Do you want to overwrite it with the latest Microsoft Project format?

• To overwrite it, click Yes.

• To save it in the Microsoft Project 98 format, click No.

[Yes] [No] [Cancel]

If you need to save your project files in Project 98 format for compatibility, you can set a default in Tools> Options>Save>Save files as.

4 If you save it in Project 98 format you will receive a further dialog box warning you that some features may be lost on conversion. Click OK to continue with the Save.

Step 4 – Hand It Over

Once the project is completed, the project manager's role is finished. However, some project managers have problems with this final step.

First, you have to let go and let the people who will be responsible for the ongoing operation take over managing the process. They won't like it or feel comfortable if you are peering over their shoulders the whole time, so let them get on with it. You should have planned any required training and, once they are up to speed, they will be fine.

But, second, you cannot just dump the new process on them. As mentioned above, you should have planned any necessary training for them, but they will almost certainly have some problems adapting to new ways of doing things. What you must do is be available if they need you. This means scheduling some of your time to support the people carrying out the new process. This should only be for an initial, short, critical period (usually in the region of a month).

The hand-over time is a great opportunity to finish off any outstanding paperwork or documentation. Tidy up the project files and back everything up.

The last scheduled task on the project should be to arrange and hold a post-implementation review. This is the time when you can go right back to the original objectives and see if they have been achieved or not. Was there anything that happened during the project that could not be dealt with or included in the project? If there was, should another project be initiated to deal with it?

As part of this review, the methods and tools used on the project should also be examined, and anything learned should be noted for the benefit of future projects (your own, or those of anyone else in the organization).

Last but not least, don't forget to thank everyone who helped you with the project: they will appreciate it. One of the nicest ways of thanking the project team is to take them out for a project team celebration meal.

Tasks and Milestones

Tasks represent the basic building blocks of a project and milestones are the reference points we use to measure progress. In this chapter, we will use these to form the basic project plan.

Covers

Chapter Four

Project Tasks

Project tasks are the basic building blocks of a project plan. They represent the pieces of work that have to be done in order to carry out the project.

A project could be treated as just one very large task, but there would be two problems with this:

1. It would be very difficult to estimate and schedule the effort required to carry it out. By breaking a project down into a number of smaller tasks, you will be able to estimate more accurately how long each will take and therefore how long the project will take in total.

2. It would be very difficult to control it and measure progress until the project was complete. By splitting it into tasks you can track progress by the completion of individual tasks.

So split your project down into tasks that you can estimate, schedule and control.

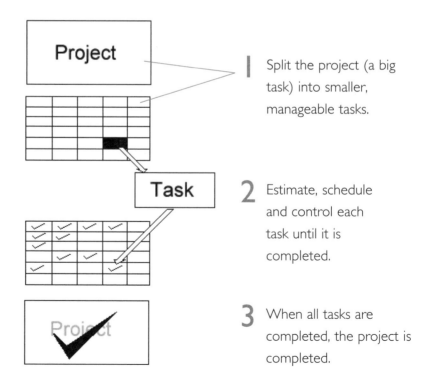

1 Split the project (a big task) into smaller, manageable tasks.

2 Estimate, schedule and control each task until it is completed.

3 When all tasks are completed, the project is completed.

Creating a Task

Although you will need to build up all the tasks involved in a project, it is very unlikely that you will be able to identify them all at the start. So to begin with you should just put in any key tasks that you have identified.

Tasks can be entered in any view that includes Task Name, but the Gantt Chart view (which is the default view) is the easiest one to use to build up your Task List.

1 Open your project file, hide Project Guide and switch to Gantt Chart view (if you are not already in it).

2 Click in the Task Name field.

3 Type "Agree Project Objectives" and press Enter.

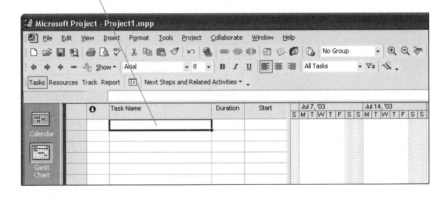

A Task ID (1) is automatically assigned and the default task duration of 1 day is allocated. The "?" after the duration indicates that it is an estimated duration at this stage.

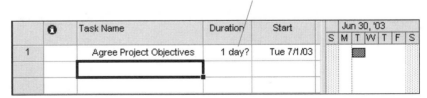

4 Click the Save button on the Toolbar to save the project.

Task Duration

One of the main reasons for breaking a project down into tasks is to be able to estimate the amount of work effort required to complete it.

While it is easier to estimate the work effort involved in a small piece of work than a large piece you may still not know what's involved. So what can you base your estimate on?

The bigger the task the more unknown factors there will be, so increase your estimate to allow for this.

- *Experience* – if you've done something similar before, how long did it take?

- *Advice* – if you know someone who's done something similar, how long did it take them?

- *Guidelines* – does your organization have any guidelines available for you to use?

- *Guess* – if none of the other options are available, your guess is probably as good as anyone else's!

Whatever method you use, it is worth getting someone else to check it. Two heads really are better than one when it comes to estimating.

All new tasks are automatically created with an estimated duration of 1 day by default. This is indicated by a "?" after the duration. Once you enter a duration the "?" is removed to show it is no longer an estimate. If, however, you are still not certain about the estimate you can enter any new value with a "?" to keep it as an estimate.

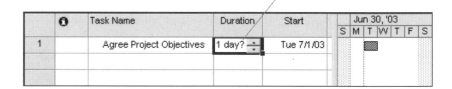

This is a useful feature as you can easily spot the estimated durations and even select them using a filter (filters are covered in a later topic).

You can change the task duration using the spin controls:

1 Click on the Duration for Task 1 and use the spin controls to increase or reduce it.

	❶	Task Name	Duration	Start	Jun 30, '03					
					S	M	T	W	T	F
1		Agree Project Objectives	2 days	Tue 7/1/03					▨	

Notice that as soon as you change the duration the "?" disappears as it is no longer an estimated duration.

You can also change the duration by typing in the Duration field. If you just type a number it defaults to days – to use another unit you need to type it in after the number.

	❶	Task Name	Duration	Start	Jun 30, '03					
					S	M	T	W	T	F
1		Agree Project Objectives	24 hrs	Tue 7/1/03					▨	

2 To change the duration time unit, type the number of Units followed by m (min), h (hrs), d (day), w (wk) or mo (month).

You can enter task duration as either Working Time (the default) or Elapsed Time. Working Time will be scheduled according to the Resources available to carry out the work, while Elapsed Time will be scheduled based on calendar days.

Notice above that 24 hours have been scheduled to take 3 working days (Tuesday to Thursday) while (below) 24 hours' elapsed time will be scheduled as one day:

For elapsed time type an "e" in front of the type (em, eh, ed, ew or emo).

	❶	Task Name	Duration	Start	Jun 30, '03					
					S	M	T	W	T	F
1		Agree Project Objectives	24 ehrs	Tue 7/1/03				▨		

Adding Tasks

To add additional tasks at the end of an existing Task List, do the following:

1 Click on the first blank Task Name.

2 Type in "Identify Project Team". In Duration type "2" and press Enter.

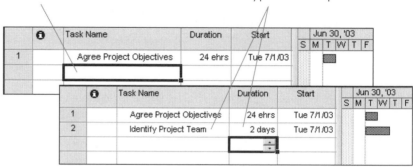

3 Now type in the following tasks and durations:

Produce Outline Project Plan	1d
Identify Business Case	2d
Analyze the Risks	1d

You can also use the Insert key as a short cut to insert a task.

4 To insert a task into an existing Task List, click the Task Name for Task 2 (Identify Project Team) and select Insert>New Task from the Menu Bar.

If any task names do not fit into the field, double-click on the Task Name column header and select "best fit".

5 Type in "Identify Stakeholders" and press Enter. Remember to save your project.

Task Dependencies

When you first identify your key tasks you should sequence them in the order that they will need to happen:

	❶	Task Name	Duration	Start	Jun 30, '03 S M T W T F S
1		Agree Project Objectives	1 day	Tue 7/1/03	
2		Identify Stakeholders	1 day?	Tue 7/1/03	
3		Identify Project Team	2 days	Tue 7/1/03	
4		Produce Outline Project Plan	1 day	Tue 7/1/03	
5		Identify Business Case	2 days	Tue 7/1/03	
6		Analyze the Risks	1 day	Tue 7/1/03	

It looks from the above as though all the tasks will happen at the same time but that is not the way things usually happen in a project. Tasks are usually dependent on input from other tasks and other tasks are usually dependent on them.

Typically, Task 3 cannot begin until Task 2 has been completed...

...and once Task 3 has been completed, Task 4 can begin.

In Project 2002 you create these dependencies by linking tasks. Linking allows you to specify those circumstances where the start or finish of a task is dependent on the start or finish of another.

The most common type of dependency or link is the finish-to-start dependency (as illustrated above) where the finish of Task 2 allows Task 3 to begin.

However there are three other types of link:

Start-to-start   Task 3 can start at the same time as Task 2.

Finish-to-finish   Task 3 must finish when Task 2 finishes.

Start-to-finish   when Task 2 starts Task 3 must finish.

But these are likely to be the exception rather than the rule.

Linking Tasks

Task dependencies are created by linking tasks.

The default dependency for linking tasks is a finish-to-start dependency and this will normally be the dependency you want for most tasks in a project. It is easiest to link all the tasks in a project in this way to start with and then make any changes to nonstandard links afterwards.

1 Click on the Task Name column header to select all of the tasks in the project.

You can also select tasks by dragging across the Task IDs or Task Names.

	ⓘ	Task Name	Duration	Start	Jun 30, '03 S M T W T F S
1		Agree Project Objectives	1 day	Tue 7/1/03	
2		Identify Stakeholders	1 day?	Tue 7/1/03	
3		Identify Project Team	2 days	Tue 7/1/03	
4		Produce Outline Project Plan	1 day	Tue 7/1/03	
5		Identify Business Case	2 days	Tue 7/1/03	
6		Analyze the Risks	1 day	Tue 7/1/03	

2 Click the Link Tasks button on the Toolbar:

	ⓘ	Task Name	Duration	Start	Jun 30, '03 S M T W T F S	Jul 7, '03 S M T W T F S
1		Agree Project Objectives	1 day	Tue 7/1/03		
2		Identify Stakeholders	1 day?	Wed 7/2/03		
3		Identify Project Team	2 days	Thu 7/3/03		
4		Produce Outline Project Plan	1 day	Mon 7/7/03		
5		Identify Business Case	2 days	Tue 7/8/03		
6		Analyze the Risks	1 day	Thu 7/10/03		

The tasks are linked in a finish-to-start dependency.

Get into the habit of saving your project after each topic or change. Then if anything goes wrong you can always go back to the saved version.

You can select individual tasks to link by holding down Ctrl and clicking the individual Task Names or Task IDs.

3 Save your project. It is a good idea to save your project after completing each topic or after making any changes unless something has gone wrong.

Unlinking Tasks

Once you have linked all the tasks in the project you may need to unlink some.

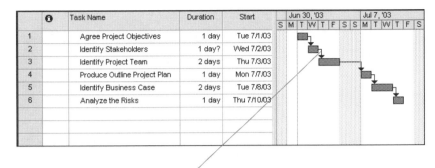

Double-click the link between Task 2 (Identify Stakeholders) and Task 3 (Identify Project Team). The Task Dependency dialog box opens:

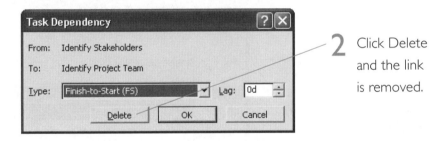

2 Click Delete and the link is removed.

To unlink several tasks, you can also drag across them to select them.

3 You can also unlink tasks by holding down Ctrl, clicking on the tasks and then clicking the Unlink button on the Toolbar:

Changing Dependencies

Although the majority of tasks in a project will normally be in a finish-to-start dependency, you may need to change some to other types of dependencies:

1 Re-establish the dependency between Task 2 (Identify Stakeholders) and Task 3 (Identify Project Team) by selecting the tasks and clicking the Link Tasks button on the Toolbar.

2 Double-click the link between Task 5 (Identify Business Case) and Task 6 (Analyze the Risks) and the Task Dependency dialog box opens.

3 Click the arrow to the right of Type.

These four dependency types were defined in "Task Dependencies" on page 57.

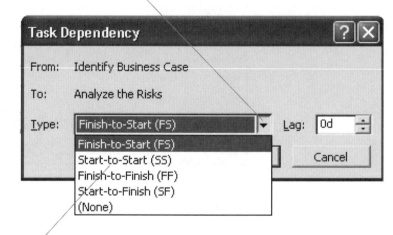

4 Select Start-to-Start and click OK. The tasks are now rescheduled to start on the same day:

	🛈	Task Name	Duration	Start	Jun 30, '03								Jul 7, '03						
					S	M	T	W	T	F	S	S	M	T	W	T	F	S
1		Agree Project Objectives	1 day	Tue 7/1/03														
2		Identify Stakeholders	1 day?	Wed 7/2/03														
3		Identify Project Team	2 days	Thu 7/3/03														
4		Produce Outline Project Plan	1 day	Mon 7/7/03														
5		Identify Business Case	2 days	Tue 7/8/03														
6		Analyze the Risks	1 day	Tue 7/8/03														

5 Save your project now before continuing with the remaining steps in this topic and do not save it at the end of the topic.

6 Double-click the link between Task 2 (Identify Stakeholders) and Task 3 (Identify Project Team) and when the Task Dependency dialog box opens select "Finish-to-Finish (FF)" as the dependency type and click OK.

	☉	Task Name	Duration	Start	
1		Agree Project Objectives	1 day	Tue 7/1/03	
2		Identify Stakeholders	1 day?	Wed 7/2/03	
3		Identify Project Team	2 days	Tue 7/1/03	
4		Produce Outline Project Plan	1 day	Thu 7/3/03	
5		Identify Business Case	2 days	Fri 7/4/03	
6		Analyze the Risks	1 day	Fri 7/4/03	

Note what has happened to Task 3. As it is dependent on Task 2 with a finish-to-finish dependency, it has to finish at the same time as Task 2. As it has 2 days' duration (work effort), Project 2002 has rescheduled it to start one day earlier than Task 2 so that it can still finish at the same time.

7 Now change the dependency between Task 4 (Produce Outline Project Plan) and Task 5 (Identify Business Case) to a "Start-to-Finish (SF)" type and see what happens.

The use of start-to-finish dependencies is best avoided. It is easier to reverse the sequence of the tasks and use a standard finish-to-start dependency.

	☉	Task Name	Duration	Start	
1		Agree Project Objectives	1 day	Tue 7/1/03	
2		Identify Stakeholders	1 day?	Wed 7/2/03	
3		Identify Project Team	2 days	Tue 7/1/03	
4		Produce Outline Project Plan	1 day	Thu 7/3/03	
5		Identify Business Case	2 days	Tue 7/1/03	
6		Analyze the Risks	1 day	Tue 7/1/03	

Project 2002 has now rescheduled Task 5 so that it finishes when Task 4 starts. This is a very unusual dependency type.

Moving a Task

If you need to move a task to a new position in the Task List, the easiest way is to use drag-and-drop. Select the ID of the task (or tasks) you want to move and then drag them to their new position.

1 Click the Task ID for Task 4 (Produce Outline Project Plan) to select it. Make sure you release the mouse button.

Make sure you select the Task ID or you may only move the selected fields and not the whole task.

	ⓘ	Task Name	Duration	Start	
1		Agree Project Objectives	1 day	Tue 7/1/03	
2		Identify Stakeholders	1 day?	Wed 7/2/03	
3		Identify Project Team	2 days	Thu 7/3/03	
4		Produce Outline Project Plan	1 day	Mon 7/7/03	
5		Identify Business Case	2 days	Tue 7/8/03	
6		Analyze the Risks	1 day	Tue 7/8/03	

2 Click the task ID again (don't release the mouse button) and drag the task to after task 6 (Analyze the Risks). Notice the insertion point marker as you drag.

5	Identify Business Case	2 days
6	Analyze the Risks	1 day

3 Release the mouse button. The task moves to its new position, its links are removed and the tasks are renumbered:

	ⓘ	Task Name	Duration	Start	
1		Agree Project Objectives	1 day	Tue 7/1/03	
2		Identify Stakeholders	1 day?	Wed 7/2/03	
3		Identify Project Team	2 days	Thu 7/3/03	
4		Identify Business Case	2 days	Mon 7/7/03	
5		Analyze the Risks	1 day	Mon 7/7/03	
6		Produce Outline Project Plan	1 day	Tue 7/1/03	

4 Select Tasks 4 and 6 and click the Link Tasks button on the Toolbar. Then do the same with Tasks 5 and 6 and finally save your project.

Deleting a Task

If you need to delete a task from the Task List, simply select it and delete it.

1 Select Task 2 (Identify Stakeholders) by clicking on its Task ID.

	❶	Task Name	Duration	Start	Jun 30, '03	Jul 7, '03
					S M T W T F S	S M T W T F S
1		Agree Project Objectives	1 day	Tue 7/1/03		
2		Identify Stakeholders	1 day?	Wed 7/2/03		
3		Identify Project Team	2 days	Thu 7/3/03		
4		Identify Business Case	2 days	Mon 7/7/03		
5		Analyze the Risks	1 day	Mon 7/7/03		
6		Produce Outline Project Plan	1 day	Wed 7/9/03		

2 Click Edit>Delete Task on the Menu Bar. The task is removed from the project:

	❶	Task Name	Duration	Start	Jun 30, '03	Jul 7, '03
					S M T W T F S	S M T W T F S
1		Agree Project Objectives	1 day	Tue 7/1/03		
2		Identify Project Team	2 days	Wed 7/2/03		
3		Identify Business Case	2 days	Fri 7/4/03		
4		Analyze the Risks	1 day	Fri 7/4/03		
5		Produce Outline Project Plan	1 day	Tue 7/8/03		

When you have used the Undo button it turns into the Redo button to allow you to cancel the Undo.

3 If you delete the wrong task (or tasks) in error you can always reverse your last action. Click on the Undo button on the Toolbar.

Project only lets you undo or redo the last action.

4 You can also delete fields or whole tasks with the Delete key. Click on the task name for Task 5 (Analyze the Risks) and press the Delete key. The Smart Tag pops up giving you the option to delete the name or whole task. Click the Undo button to cancel.

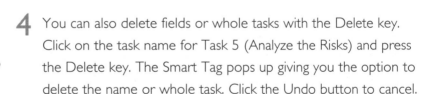

4		Identify Business Case	2 days	Mon 7/7/03
5	✕ ▾		1 day	Mon 7/7/03
6				Wed 7/9/03
	⦿	Only clear the contents of Task Name Cell		
	○	Delete the entire task		

The Task Form

Task Entry view is one of the additional views that is available in Project 2002. You can use it to view, enter and edit details of individual tasks.

If the View Bar is not currently displayed you can get it back with View>View Bar on the Menu Bar.

1 Click the down arrow at the bottom of the View Bar until More Views appears.

2 Click More Views.

3 Scroll down through the More Views list, select Task Entry and click Apply. The Task Form is displayed in the bottom half of the view.

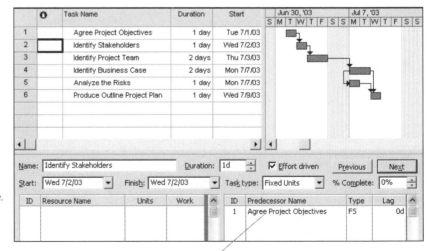

You can drag the split bar up and down to change the top and bottom pane size.

4 You can now view, enter and edit task details directly in the lower pane. You can also double-click the split bar to get back to Gantt Chart view.

Project Milestones

Project milestones are the key events that mark a project's progress.

The simplest way of inserting a milestone is to enter a task with a zero duration.

1 Click on the blank Task Name below Task 6 (Produce Outline Project Plan).

2 Type "Project Approval", press Tab, type "0" and press Enter. A milestone is inserted into the project plan.

3 Link Task 6 (Produce Outline Project Plan) and Task 7 (the milestone) by selecting them and clicking the Link Tasks button on the Toolbar.

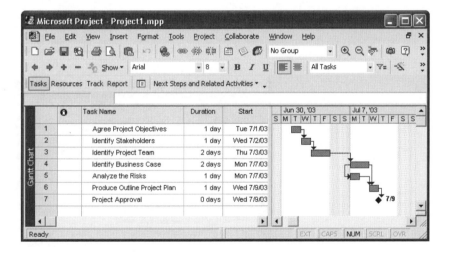

4 Click the Duration, type "5d" and double-click the task. The Task Information dialog box opens.

5 Click the Advanced tab, click the Mark Task as Milestone checkbox (bottom left) and click OK. The task changes back to a milestone but the duration stays as 5 days.

Recurring Tasks

Any task that is repeated within a project is called a recurring task. It could be a regular project team meeting, a review with your project sponsor or production of a monthly management report.

1 To insert a recurring task, click in an empty Task Name field.

2 Click Insert>Recurring Task on the Menu Bar and the Recurring Task Information box appears.

3 Type "Project Team Meeting"; type "1h"; select "Weekly"; select "Thursday"; and click OK.

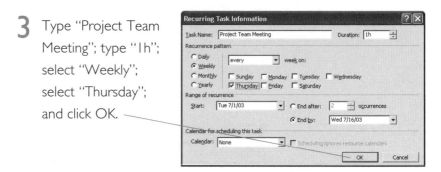

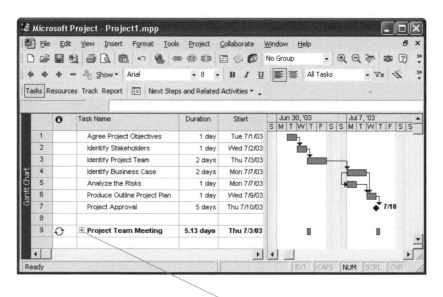

The recurring task is inserted. Click the "+" next to the Task Name to show the individual meetings. Note also the duration is 5.13 days (the two meetings and the time between them).

Adding Structure

In this chapter, we begin to add some structure to the project by developing summary tasks and subtasks and using outlining.

Covers

Chapter Five

Project Structure

A simple project, like carrying out and presenting a strategy study, might consist of as little as a dozen tasks. A medium-sized project, such as building a house or implementing a computer system, could run into over a hundred individual tasks. A very large project could run into thousands of tasks.

If you try to identify and plan for every individual task right from the outset you will almost certainly be doomed to failure. In the early stages of a project there will usually be a large number of unknown factors. These factors will only become known as the project progresses. To cope with this you need to break a project down into manageable chunks, one level at a time. This is usually referred to as a Work Breakdown Structure and represented hierarchically:

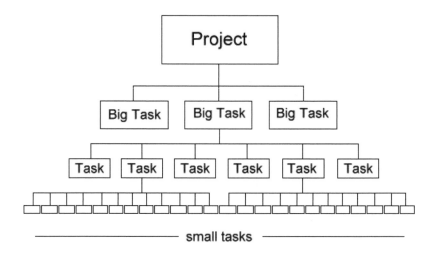

1   Break the project down into some discrete chunks (big tasks) with deliverables.

2   As you begin each big task, break it down into its individual tasks.

3   As you begin to work on each task, break it down into its individual subtasks (if relevant).

So when you first start a project you need to break it down into the first-level major chunks (big tasks). Going back to our 4-step approach to carrying out a project, we could use that as a basis for our big chunks. That would give us the following four steps as our first-level big tasks:

1. Define the objectives.

2. Plan the project.

3. Carry it out.

4. Hand it over.

You would then start to identify the tasks required to carry out Step 1 (defining the objectives) before worrying about the detailed tasks involved in Step 2.

As you get towards the end of defining the objectives you would then start to identify and plan the detailed tasks in the next step (planning the project) and so on.

Working through the project in this manner means that there will be fewer unknown factors when you come to identify the tasks and estimate the effort involved in them.

In Project 2002, the process of structuring your project plan in this way is called Outlining. The Outlining buttons are on the Formatting Toolbar when in Gantt Chart view:

The Outlining buttons are also visible from within Task Sheet and Task Usage views.

Outdent   Indent   Show Subtasks

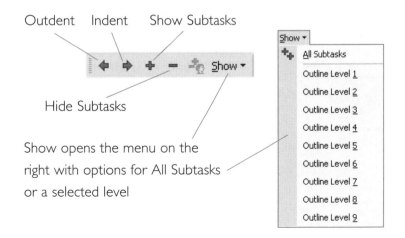

Hide Subtasks

Show opens the menu on the
right with options for All Subtasks
or a selected level

Summary Tasks

A summary task is created just like any other task, but its subtasks are indented.

1 Click Task 1 (Agree Project Objectives).

2 Click Insert>New Task on the Menu Bar (or press Insert).

3 Name the new task "Define the Objectives" and press Enter.

4 Select Tasks 2 to 8 by clicking and dragging their Task IDs and click the Indent button on the Toolbar.

	❶	Task Name	Duration	Start	Jun 30, '03	Jul 7, '03	Jul 14, '03
1		⊟ **Define the Objectives**	**12 days**	**Tue 7/1/03**			
2		Agree Project Objectives	1 day	Tue 7/1/03			
3		Identify Stakeholders	1 day	Wed 7/2/03			
4		Identify Project Team	2 days	Thu 7/3/03			
5		Identify Business Case	2 days	Mon 7/7/03			
6		Analyze the Risks	1 day	Mon 7/7/03			
7		Produce Outline Project Pla	1 day	Wed 7/9/03			
8		Project Approval	5 days	Thu 7/10/03			7/10
9							
10	↻	⊞ **Project Team Meeting**	**5.13 days**	**Thu 7/3/03**			

These tasks have now become subtasks of Task 1 (Define the Objectives) and are indented. Task 1 has become a summary task and is now shown in bold. It also has a summary bar on the right-hand side of the screen (note that it shows the 5 days for the milestone).

5 Now hide the subtasks and insert the other three steps and durations as shown below.

Hide subtasks by clicking the minus sign beside the summary task.

	❶	Task Name	Duration	Start	Jun 30, '03	Jul 7, '03	Jul 14, '03
1		⊞ **Define the Objectives**	**12 days**	**Tue 7/1/03**			
9		Plan the Project	10 days	Tue 7/1/03			
10		Carry it Out	30 days	Tue 7/1/03			
11		Hand it Over	15 days	Tue 7/1/03			
12	↻	⊞ **Project Team Meeting**	**5.13 days**	**Thu 7/3/03**			

6 Save your project.

Task Rollup

The standard way that tasks roll up into summary tasks is as a solid summary bar (as shown on the Gantt Charts on the facing page). However the project meetings are also a summary task and clicking on the plus sign beside the summary task will display the individual meetings as separate tasks. But instead of a solid line the summary line shows the individual meetings. This is a default for recurring tasks but it can be enabled individually for each task and summary task. With Project 2002 you can now set it for the whole project.

Individual tasks are enabled by double-clicking the task name and setting the "Hide task bar" and "Roll up Gantt bar" features on the General tab.

1 Open your project file and display all subtasks.

2 Select Format>Layout from the menu bar. The layout dialog box opens.

3 Select Always roll up Gantt bars and Hide Rollup bars when summary expanded.

4 Click OK. Nothing should look any different now.

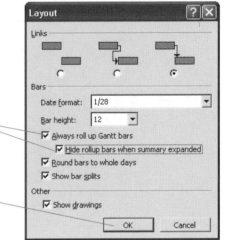

5 Now click the Show button on the menu bar and select Outline Level 1 and your project will be displayed at the top-level with rolled up rather than summary Gantt bars:

	ⓘ	Task Name	Duration	Start	Jun 30, '03 S M T W T F S	Jul 7, '03 S M T W T F S
1		⊞ **Define the Objectives**	**12 days**	**Tue 7/1/03**		
9		Plan the Project	10 days	Tue 7/1/03		
10		Carry it Out	30 days	Tue 7/1/03		
11		Hand it Over	15 days	Tue 7/1/03		
12	⟳	⊞ **Project Team Meeting**	**5.13 days**	**Thu 7/3/03**		

With this feature it is simple to change the way the whole project is displayed in summary views.

Changing the Timescale

Once you begin to link the top-level tasks on a project, they will go off the timescale in the right-hand pane and you will not be able to see the whole project. However, this is easily remedied using the Zoom In and Zoom Out buttons on the Toolbar:

1 Link the new summary tasks by selecting Tasks 1 to 11 and clicking the Link Tasks button on the Toolbar.

2 Now use the Zoom In and Zoom Out buttons on the Toolbar until you have the whole project in view again.

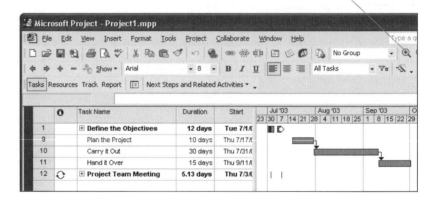

3 Now select Show All Subtasks from the Toolbar and use the Zoom In button to get back to the subtask details.

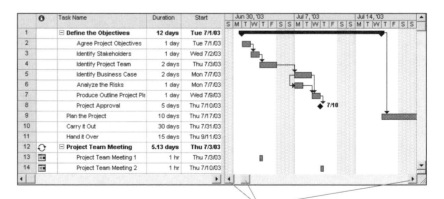

4 You may need to use the slide controls to bring the focus back to the required time period.

Project Stages

Conventionally in project management methodology, the first-level summary tasks are referred to as project stages.

Project management methodology initially grew out of the construction industry and still retains some of that industry's terminology. In later years it has also been influenced by the software development industry which, interestingly, has a lot of similarities.

Using that influence, we can now build a little further on our 4-step approach by expanding our second step (planning) into two separate stages:

- Determine what the business needs are.

- Define what we will need to do to achieve those needs.

If this sounds a bit like "overkill", keep an open mind for the time being. Hopefully, as we develop the process further, you will begin to see why we use this approach. These five project stages are conventionally referred to as:

1. *Initiation* – to define the project objectives and team structure and produce the initial project plan.

Some people refer to these project stages as project phases.

2. *Strategy* – to determine what the business needs and what the payback will be.

3. *Analysis* – to define what we will need to do in order to meet the business needs.

4. *Design and Build* – to work out how we will actually do it and then carry it out (i.e. make it, buy it, manage it, etc.).

5. *Implementation* – to install and hand over the new process and close the project.

The chief benefit of this method is that the major expense or effort usually occurs in the Design & Build stage. At each of the preceding stages you are able to reappraise the potential investment and ensure that it will still be of benefit. If it becomes questionable, the project can be wound up while costs and effort expended are still relatively low.

Implementing a 5-Stage Approach

While the 5-stage approach may indeed be overkill for a strategy study or a smaller project, somewhere between 3 and 8 stages will usually fit most projects. Start with these 5 standard stages and use whichever stages are appropriate to your project, discarding any which are not and adding any additional ones that you feel your project needs.

1 Select Task 1 (Define the Objectives) and change the Task Name to "Initiation Stage".

2 Select Task 9 (Plan the Project). Insert a new Task 9 "Strategy Stage" and outdent it, then indent Task 10 (Plan the Project).

| 9 | | ⊟ **Strategy Stage** | **10 days** | **Thu 7/17/03** |
| 10 | | Plan the Project | 10 days | Thu 7/17/03 |

To insert more than one task, drag down the Task IDs to select the required number of tasks. Press Insert.

3 Select Task 11 (Carry it Out). Insert and outdent two new tasks:

- Analysis Stage
- Design & Build Stage

4 Select Task 13 (Carry it Out) and Indent it.

5 Select Task 14 (Hand it Over), insert a new task "Implementation Stage" and outdent it, then indent Task 15 (Hand it Over).

6 Show outline level 1 and use Zoom Out to get the whole project in view. Delete Task 16 (Project Meetings) and it should look something like the following:

To switch back to summary bars, use Format> Layout from the Menu bar.

	❶	Task Name	Duration	Start	Jul '03	Aug '03	Sep '03	Oct '03
					23 30 7 14 21 28	4 11 18 25	1 8 15 22 29	6 13
1		⊞ **Initiation Stage**	12 days	Tue 7/1/03				
9		⊞ **Strategy Stage**	10 days	Thu 7/17/03				
11		Analysis Stage	1 day?	Tue 7/1/03				
12		⊞ **Design & Build Stage**	30 days	Thu 7/31/03				
14		⊞ **Implementation Stage**	15 days	Thu 9/11/03				

We have now implemented the 5-stage approach but we still need to finish it off in the next couple of sections.

Change Budgets

When you first start a project you may be able to identify some of the key tasks but there will still be a lot of unknown factors, particularly in the later stages. To cope with this, and still be able to produce an outline schedule, you need to put in some sort of allowance, a change budget.

How Much?

How much change budget should you add to cope with these unknown factors? How long is a piece of string?

While there is no right answer to this question, there is a rule of thumb that seems to work for the author for medium-sized projects (around 9 months' duration):

These amounts are based on medium-sized projects – smaller projects should require less but larger projects may need more!

- Add 100% to your initial estimate (yes, double it).

- When you get to the end of the Strategy stage and estimate the remaining work on the project, add 50%.

- Likewise, at the end of the Analysis stage add 25%.

- Finally, at the end of Design add 10%.

What you will be doing through the project is identifying more tasks. As you identify these additional tasks you can reduce your change budget accordingly. Hopefully as you reach the end of each stage your change budget figure for that stage will be down to zero. It will have done its job.

Key Tasks

Before you put in your change budget figure it is a good idea to make sure you have identified any key tasks. Then you can put them in at the same time.

If the objective of the project were to select a new computer accounting package, you would possibly have identified key tasks such as: Agree the Requirements; Select a Package; Purchase the Package; Install the Package; Train the Users; and Convert to the New Package.

In the next topic we will put these key tasks and an appropriate change budget into our project.

Adding a Change Budget

Your project should currently look something like the illustration at the bottom of page 74 (if not, enter the necessary tasks as described in "Implementing a 5-Stage Approach").

1 Click the (Show Subtasks) plus sign beside Task 9 (Strategy Stage) and change the name of Task 10 to "Change Budget".

2 Insert 4 new tasks in front of Task 12 (Design & Build Stage):

"Agree Requirements"	–	duration "5d"
"Select Package"	–	duration "5d"
"Purchase Package"	–	duration "2d"
"Change Budget"	–	duration "3d"

Link them and indent them.

3 Insert 2 new tasks in front of task 17 (Carry it Out): "Design" (10d) and "Install Package" (5d). Change "Carry it Out" to "Change Budget" (25d) and link them.

Insert 2 new tasks in front of 21 (Hand it Over): "Train Users" (5d) and "Convert to New Package" (5d). Change "Hand it Over" to "Change Budget" (10d); link and indent them if needed.

4 Show all subtasks and link the last subtask under each summary task (stage) to the first subtask in the next stage. Finally delete any stray or surplus links between stages.

You delete links by double-clicking them and then selecting Delete in the Task Dependency box.

	ⓘ	Task Name	Duration	Start	Jul '03	Aug '03	Sep '03	Oct '03	Nov '03
					23 30 7 14 21 28	4 11 18 25	1 8 15 22 29	6 13 20 27	3 10 17 24
1		⊟ Initiation Stage	12 days	Tue 7/1/03					
2		Agree Project Objectives	1 day	Tue 7/1/03					
3		Identify Stakeholders	1 day	Wed 7/2/03					
4		Identify Project Team	2 days	Thu 7/3/03					
5		Identify Business Case	2 days	Mon 7/7/03					
6		Analyze the Risks	1 day	Mon 7/7/03					
7		Produce Outline Project Plε	1 day	Wed 7/9/03					
8		Project Approval	5 days	Thu 7/10/03	7/10				
9		⊟ Strategy Stage	10 days	Thu 7/17/03					
10		Change Budget	10 days	Thu 7/17/03					
11		⊟ Analysis Stage	15 days	Thu 7/31/03					
12		Agree Requirements	5 days	Thu 7/31/03					
13		Select Package	5 days	Thu 8/7/03					
14		Purchase Package	2 days	Thu 8/14/03					
15		Change Budget	3 days	Mon 8/18/03					
16		⊟ Design & Build Stage	40 days	Thu 8/21/03					
17		Design	10 days	Thu 8/21/03					
18		Install Package	5 days	Thu 9/4/03					
19		Change Budget	25 days	Thu 9/11/03					
20		⊟ Implementation Stage	20 days	Thu 10/16/03					

Breaking Tasks Down

Having inserted summary tasks (Stages) as the first-level of the project work breakdown, their constituent tasks become the second-level. If you then need to break those tasks down into further subtasks, they become the third-level on the project Work Breakdown Structure (WBS).

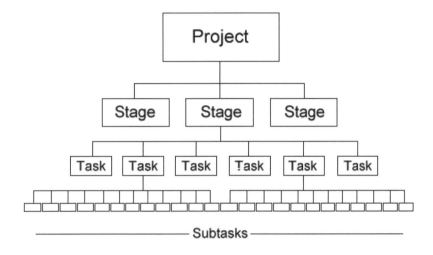

In project management methodology, these third-level subtasks are often called Activities.

So how big or small should a task be?

If you are to be able to estimate, schedule and control a task with any degree of accuracy, it needs to be small enough to allow you to do this. But it must be large enough to have some form of deliverable or product so that its completion can be confirmed. Finally, although more than one person may work on a task, only one person must be responsible for its completion.

Conventional wisdom is that a task should be between 1 and 10 days' effort (typically around 5 days). If it's bigger, then you should attempt to break it down into subtasks. If it's smaller, then see if you can combine it with some other task.

At the end of the day, it's you, as the project manager, who should make the decisions, so these and any other guidelines are just that. If you want a 20-day task and it makes sense, then have it: after all, it's your project.

Outline Numbering

For a small project with a dozen or so tasks, the Task ID is probably a good enough way of keeping track of tasks. But as your project starts to build up you will want to be able to hide and show tasks and still keep track of where everything fits. Outline numbering allows you to achieve this.

1 Click Tools>Options on the Menu Bar. The Options dialog opens.

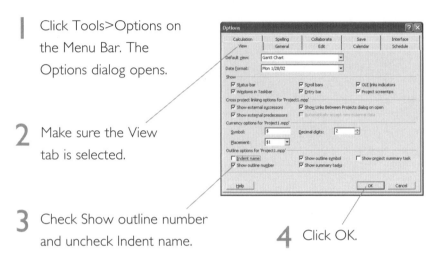

2 Make sure the View tab is selected.

3 Check Show outline number and uncheck Indent name.

4 Click OK.

5 Click Show Subtasks for Task 1 (Initiation Stage).

If any task information is hidden from view, double-click the column header and select "Best Fit".

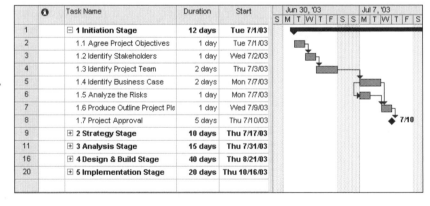

	ⓘ	Task Name	Duration	Start
1		⊟ 1 Initiation Stage	12 days	Tue 7/1/03
2		1.1 Agree Project Objectives	1 day	Tue 7/1/03
3		1.2 Identify Stakeholders	1 day	Wed 7/2/03
4		1.3 Identify Project Team	2 days	Thu 7/3/03
5		1.4 Identify Business Case	2 days	Mon 7/7/03
6		1.5 Analyze the Risks	1 day	Mon 7/7/03
7		1.6 Produce Outline Project Pla	1 day	Wed 7/9/03
8		1.7 Project Approval	5 days	Thu 7/10/03
9		⊞ 2 Strategy Stage	10 days	Thu 7/17/03
11		⊞ 3 Analysis Stage	15 days	Thu 7/31/03
16		⊞ 4 Design & Build Stage	40 days	Thu 8/21/03
20		⊞ 5 Implementation Stage	20 days	Thu 10/16/03

Your stages and tasks are now numbered in a structured format. Additional sub-subtasks below Task 1.4 will be numbered 1.4.1, 1.4.2 and so on.

Outline Codes

In addition to standard outline numbering, Project 2002 also lets you create your own custom outline codes which are held in the custom outline codes field. One or more tasks or resources (covered later) can then be assigned to the same outline code so they can be grouped together.

This feature could be useful if your project is part of a larger project or program and you are required to use standard outline codes for your tasks.

1 To define a custom outline code select Tools>Customize>Fields from the Menu bar.

2 Select the Custom Outline Codes tab.

3 Then click the Define Code Mask button. The definition box will open.

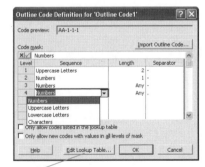

4 Now you can define each part of the code. In this case 2 uppercase letters followed by three numbers with dash separators.

5 Once you have defined your code structure, click on Edit Lookup Table.

We will look at using and displaying lookup codes later.

6 Then type in any lookup codes with their description.

Subtasks

Any task that is larger than 10 days' work effort will probably need to be split down into subtasks or the individual activities that make up the task. Even if a task is smaller than 10 days it may still be beneficial to split it down.

Activities

Third-level subtasks are often referred to as Activities. They should not be less than half a day nor more than 5 days and should be carried out by one person. For example if you have two people assigned to a large task, it should be split into (at least) two subtasks or activities, each of which is allocated to one person.

By allocating these bottom-level activities to one person it becomes easier to estimate, schedule and control them. It is easier to estimate as you can involve the person who will be doing the work. It will be easier to schedule as it only involves one person's time. And it will be easier to control as you have only one person to ask about progress.

Task Name	Duration
⊞ **1 Initiation Stage**	**12 days**
⊟ **2 Strategy Stage**	**15 days**
2.1 Carry out Interviews	4 days
2.2 Produce Draft Requirements	2 days
2.3 Feedback Sessions	1 day
2.4 Consolidate Results	1 day
2.5 Finalize Requirements	1 day
2.6 Evolve Other Recommendations	1 day
2.7 Carry out Risk Analysis	2 days
2.8 Produce Forward Plan	1 day
2.9 Report to Management	2 days
⊞ **3 Analysis Stage**	**15 days**
⊞ **4 Design & Build Stage**	**40 days**
⊞ **5 Implementation Stage**	**20 days**

1 Open your project and show subtasks for Stage 2 (Strategy).

2 Insert the 9 new tasks with their durations as shown and delete the old "Change Budget" task.

3 The new tasks should be linked; if not, link them.

4 You decide that 2 people will carry out the interviews so insert 2 new tasks after 2.1.

⊟ **2 Strategy Stage**	**15 days**
2.1 Carry out Interviews	4 days
2.2 Produce Draft Requirements	2 days

5 Type in the two new subtasks and their durations as shown (don't worry about the outline numbers).

⊟ 2 Strategy Stage	19 days
2.1 Carry out Interviews	4 days
2.2 Interview Managers	2 days
2.3 Interview Staff	2 days
2.4 Produce Draft Requirements	2 days

6 Select the two subtasks and indent them. Notice that Task 2.1 ("Carry out interviews") has now become a summary task (with a "–" beside it) and the two new subtasks are now numbered 2.1.1 and 2.1.2.

Task Name	Duration	Start
⊞ 1 Initiation Stage	12 days	Tue 7/1/03
⊟ 2 Strategy Stage	15 days	Thu 7/17/03
⊟ 2.1 Carry out Interviews	4 days	Thu 7/17/03
2.1.1 Interview Managers	2 days	Thu 7/17/03
2.1.2 Interview Staff	2 days	Mon 7/21/03
2.2 Produce Draft Requirements	2 days	Wed 7/23/03
2.3 Feedback Sessions	1 day	Fri 7/25/03
2.4 Consolidate Results	1 day	Mon 7/28/03
2.5 Finalize Requirements	1 day	Tue 7/29/03
2.6 Evolve Other Recommendations	1 day	Wed 7/30/03
2.7 Carry out Risk Analysis	2 days	Thu 7/31/03
2.8 Produce Forward Plan	1 day	Mon 8/4/03
2.9 Report to Management	2 days	Tue 8/5/03
⊞ 3 Analysis Stage	15 days	Thu 8/7/03
⊞ 4 Design & Build Stage	40 days	Thu 8/28/03
⊞ 5 Implementation Stage	20 days	Thu 10/23/03

7 Hide the two new subtasks by clicking the "–" beside 2.1.

Task Name	Duration	Start
⊞ 1 Initiation Stage	12 days	Tue 7/1/03
⊟ 2 Strategy Stage	15 days	Thu 7/17/03
⊞ 2.1 Carry out Interviews	4 days	Thu 7/17/03
2.2 Produce Draft Requirements	2 days	Wed 7/23/03
2.3 Feedback Sessions	1 day	Fri 7/25/03
2.4 Consolidate Results	1 day	Mon 7/28/03
2.5 Finalize Requirements	1 day	Tue 7/29/03
2.6 Evolve Other Recommendations	1 day	Wed 7/30/03
2.7 Carry out Risk Analysis	2 days	Thu 7/31/03

Stages, Tasks and Activities

Summarizing the content of this chapter, we have split a project down hierarchically into three levels: Stages, Tasks and Activities. This is the Work Breakdown Structure:

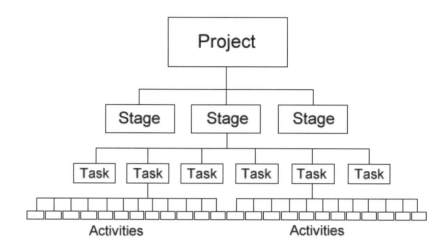

Stages

Stages are the first (top) level summary tasks that define the structure of the project. The typical project will have around five or six of these main stages. In Project 2002 we set these up as summary tasks.

Tasks

Tasks are the basic building blocks of the project. Typically, a task will be about 5 days' work effort and will have some sort of deliverable. It will also have dependencies (it will be dependent on another task).

Activities

Activities are the third-level (detailed subtasks) of a project. Larger tasks will be split down into activities to enable the project manager to allocate, schedule and control the work. Activities will still have some sort of deliverable but will be carried out by one person.

By structuring your project this way and reflecting it in your project plan, you will be able to manage and communicate your project in the most effective way to your project sponsor, project team and any other stakeholders.

More About Tasks

This chapter goes into tasks in a little more detail. It covers lag and lead times, task notes, setting deadline dates, the critical path and splitting and moving tasks.

Covers

Chapter Six

Lag Time and Lead Time

Up to now we have been linking tasks, mainly in a finish-to-start dependency, with the next task starting immediately after the preceding task finishes. However, there are times when you will want the tasks to overlap or have a gap between them.

Lag Time

Lag time is when there is a gap (or lag) between the finish of one task and the start of the next task.

Lead Time

Lead time is when there is an overlap, with the next task starting before the previous one has finished. In Project 2002, these are both specified using the Lag field (a positive number being lag time and a negative number being lead time).

 Use Zoom In and Out on the Toolbar to alter the timescale if necessary.

| Show the subtasks in the Initiation stage of the project.

 Note that we set the Project Approval (milestone) with a 5-day duration to allow for the approval decision although there was not 5 days' work involved.

Task Name	Duration	Start	Jun 30, '03	Jul 7, '03
			S M T W T F S S	M T W T F S
⊟ **1 Initiation Stage**	**12 days**	**Tue 7/1/03**		
1.1 Agree Project Objectives	1 day	Tue 7/1/03		
1.2 Identify Stakeholders	1 day	Wed 7/2/03		
1.3 Identify Project Team	2 days	Thu 7/3/03		
1.4 Identify Business Case	2 days	Mon 7/7/03		
1.5 Analyze the Risks	1 day	Mon 7/7/03		
1.6 Produce Outline Project Plan	1 day	Wed 7/9/03		
1.7 Project Approval	5 days	Thu 7/10/03		◆ 7/10
⊞ **2 Strategy Stage**	**15 days**	**Thu 7/17/03**		

2 Double-click the link between 1.6 (Produce Outline Plan) and 1.7 (Project Approval). The Task Dependency dialog box opens.

3 Change the Lag to "5d" and then click OK.

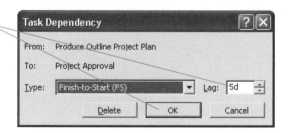

4 Change the Duration of 1.7 (Project Approval) back to zero. The schedule shows the correct milestone date with the 5-day lag:

Now let's look at putting in lead time:

1 Double-click the link between 1.3 (Identify Project Team) and 1.4 (Identify Business Case) to open the Task Dependency dialog.

2 Click the down arrow spinner control to produce a Lag of "-1" and click OK.

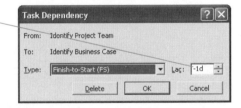

You can also change the lag time by double-clicking on the dependent task and altering Lag time in the Task Information dialog box, Predecessors tab.

There is now a 1-day overlap between 1.3 (Identify Project Team) and 1.4 (Identify Business Case). As we had already set the link between 1.4 (Identify Business Case) and 1.5 (Analyze the Risks) to a start-to-start dependency, task 1.5 has been brought back with task 1.4 so this task is now overlapped as well. As a consequence, we have also brought the project approval forward by one day.

Task Notes

You can add notes to a task in Gantt Chart view or any other Task view where the information box is displayed.

1 Open your project in Gantt Chart view.

2 Select Task 1.6 (Produce Outline Project Plan).

3 Click the Task Note button on the Toolbar. The Task Information dialog box opens with the Notes tab selected.

4 Type in your note: "Need to confirm report format for the Outline Plan" and click OK.

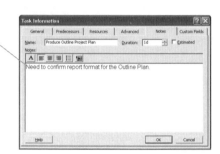

5 Pause the mouse pointer over the note and the note will pop-up on the screen:

Information box   Task Note button

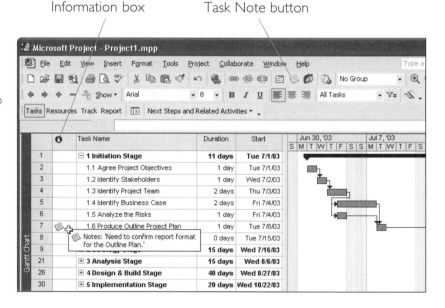

Double-click the Note Indicator to edit the note.

The Note Indicator (yellow note symbol) is displayed in the Information field for the task.

Deadline Dates

Tasks can include a deadline date that allows an indicator to be displayed if a task is going to finish after its deadline. Deadline dates have little impact on the actual scheduling and should not be confused with task constraints (which we will see in a later topic) which can determine when a task will actually be scheduled.

Deadline dates are set on the Advanced tab of the Task Information dialog box.

1   Open your project in Gantt Chart view and double-click on Task 1.2 (Identify Stakeholders). Select the Advanced tab on the Task Information dialog box.

2   Click on the Deadline down arrow to get a calendar and select a date earlier than the current scheduled date. Then click OK.

3   The task now has a warning indicator in the indicator column. Move your cursor over the indicator and the warning message will appear.

Because Project 2002 will reschedule tasks as things change, it is a good idea to set deadline dates on any relevant tasks.

ⓘ	Task Name	Duration	Start	Jun 30, '03
				S M T W T F S
	⊟ **1 Initiation Stage**	**11 days**	**Tue 7/1/03**	
	1.1 Agree Project Objectives	1 day	Tue 7/1/03	
❗⊕	1.2 Identify Stakeholders	1 day	Wed 7/2/03	
❗	This task finishes on Wed 7/2/03 which is later than its Deadline on Tue 7/1/03	2 days	Thu 7/3/03	
		2 days	Fri 7/4/03	
	1.5 Analyze the Risks	1 day	Fri 7/4/03	
▨	1.6 Produce Outline Project Plan	1 day	Tue 7/8/03	
	1.7 Project Approval	0 days	Tue 7/15/03	

Note that the Task bar on the Gantt Chart to the right now has a small green arrow indicating the deadline.

Moving Around

As your project file starts to build up, you will not be able to get all the detailed information in one view at a time.

Scrollbars

You can use the scrollbars to scroll the view horizontally and vertically. The Gantt Chart view has one vertical scrollbar which moves the task information and timescale in step. It also has two horizontal scrollbars so that you can move through the task information independently of the timescale.

Vertical slider

When you use the vertical scrollbar slider the task numbers are displayed in a pop-up box.

You can drag the divider between the Task list and Gantt Chart to the left or right to get the desired amount of information on the screen.

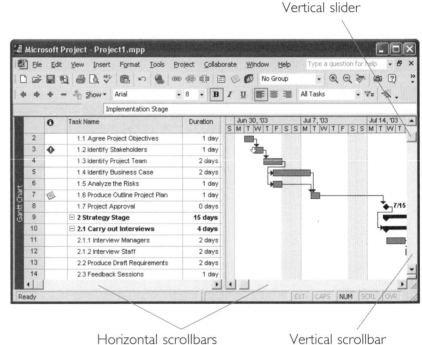

Horizontal scrollbars   Vertical scrollbar

Go To Selected Task

You can also use the Go To Selected Task button on the Toolbar to bring any task into view in the timescale:

1   Click on Task 15 (Consolidate Results).

2   Click the Go To Selected Task button on the Toolbar: (The timescale scrolls to the selected task.)

The Critical Path

The Critical Path is the term given to the sequence of tasks that are critical to the duration of the project. A Critical Task is one that, if delayed or lengthened, will directly affect the project finish date.

The following diagram represents a simple project consisting of four tasks. Tasks A, B and D are each of two days' duration, while Task C is of one day's duration. Tasks B and C are both dependent on Task A with finish-to-start relationships. Task D is dependent on both Tasks B and C, again with finish-to-start relationships. Assuming no lag time the total duration of the project is six days.

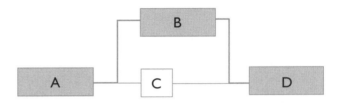

Non-critical Tasks
Even if task C were to slip by one day it would still not impact the completion of Task D and therefore the project would still be completed in six days. Task C is therefore deemed to be a non-critical Task.

Critical Tasks
On the other hand, if any of Tasks A, B or D were to slip by one day the project would take seven days to complete and these tasks are therefore deemed to be Critical Tasks.

Critical Path
The Critical Path is the path through the project that links all of the Critical Tasks. In the diagram above, the Critical Path (shown as a heavier line and shaded boxes) consists of Task A, the link between Task A and Task B, Task B, the link between Task B and Task D, and finally Task D.

Calculating the Critical Path
In Project 2002 the Critical Path is calculated by the Gantt Chart Wizard which is covered in the next topic.

Gantt Chart Wizard

The Critical Path through the project is calculated by the Gantt Chart Wizard. The default is that it will display the Critical Path and Critical Tasks in red and non-Critical Tasks and path in blue.

1 In Gantt Chart view, click the Gantt Chart Wizard button. The Wizard dialog appears.

2 Click Next and the Wizard asks you what type of information you want to display in your Gantt Chart.

3 Select Critical Path and click Next. The Wizard asks you what type of information you want to display with your Gantt bars.

There are a lot more options available in the Gantt Chart Wizard. To see what they are, select Custom Gantt Chart at Step 3.

4 Select Resources and Dates and click Next. The Wizard asks you if you want to show link lines between dependent tasks.

5 Select Yes to display links and click Next. The Wizard tells you it is ready to format.

6 Click the Format It button. The Wizard tells you that your Gantt Chart is finished.

7 Click the Exit Wizard button. The Gantt Chart is now reformatted.

Non-Critical Task (blue)   Critical Path (red)

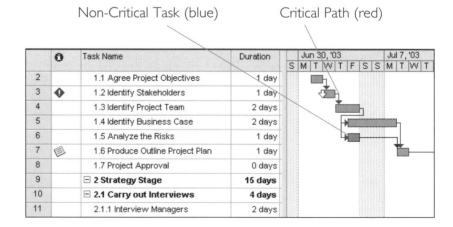

	❶	Task Name	Duration	Jun 30, '03	Jul 7, '03
2		1.1 Agree Project Objectives	1 day		
3	◆	1.2 Identify Stakeholders	1 day		
4		1.3 Identify Project Team	2 days		
5		1.4 Identify Business Case	2 days		
6		1.5 Analyze the Risks	1 day		
7	📝	1.6 Produce Outline Project Plan	1 day		
8		1.7 Project Approval	0 days		
9		⊟ 2 Strategy Stage	15 days		
10		⊟ 2.1 Carry out Interviews	4 days		
11		2.1.1 Interview Managers	2 days		

Splitting Tasks

Normally, a task will be worked on from start to finish. However, a task can be split if it needs to be interrupted and finished later.

We have a Task 2.1.1: "Interview Managers". If some of the managers were going to be away at a conference, you would need to reschedule part of this task for their return.

1 Select Task 2.1.1 (Interview Managers).

2 Click the Split Task button on the Toolbar. A pop-up asks you to select the split point.

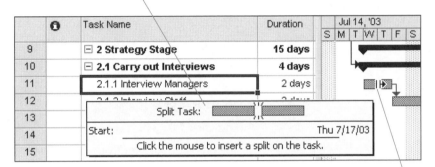

3 Position the pointer in the middle of the Gantt bar for the task and click. The task is split and a gap of one day is opened.

4 Drag the right-hand half of the task along to the next Monday and release it:

	❶	Task Name	Duration	Jul 14, '03							Jul 21, '03						
				S	M	T	W	T	F	S	S	M	T	W	T	F	S
9		⊟ 2 Strategy Stage	17 days														
10		⊟ 2.1 Carry out Interviews	6 days														
11		2.1.1 Interview Managers	2 days														
12		2.1.2 Interview Staff	2 days														
13		2.2 Produce Draft Requirements	2 days														
14		2.3 Feedback Sessions	1 day														
15		2.4 Consolidate Results	1 day														
16		2.5 Finalize Requirements	1 day														

The task is now split with a dotted line showing the link between the two halves.

Moving Linked Tasks

When you split the task in the previous topic you left a gap in the Gantt Chart. It would make sense to bring the following task (Interview Staff) forward to fill this gap:

	ⓘ	Task Name	Duration	Jul 14, '03	Jul 21, '03
				S M T W T F S	S M T W T F S
10		⊟ **2.1 Carry out Interviews**	**6 days**		
11		2.1.1 Interview Managers	2 days		
12		2.1.2 Interview Staff	2 days		
13		2.2 Produce Draft Requirements	2 days		

1 Position the mouse pointer over the Interview Staff Gantt Chart bar. The pointer changes into a Move pointer: ✛

2 Drag the Task bar back to start after the first half of Interview Managers and release the key. A Planning Wizard appears telling you that the link "cannot be honored".

3 Select Remove the link... and click OK. The tasks are unlinked and a new Critical Path is established.

4 Select 2.1.1 (Interview Managers) and 2.2 (Produce Draft Requirements) and click the Link Tasks button to re-establish the Critical Path. Note that a Calendar icon has been placed in the information column. Position your cursor over it.

A calendar note has been added to the task with a "Start No Earlier Than" constraint as we forced it to this date by moving it. We will deal with constraints in a later topic.

	ⓘ	Task Name	Duration	Jul 14, '03	Jul 21, '03
				S M T W T F S	S M T W T
7	✎	1.6 Produce Outline Project Plan	1 day		
8		1.7 Project Approval	0 days	7/15	
9		⊟ **2 Strategy Stage**	**15 days**		
10		⊟ **2.1 Carry out Interviews**	**4 days**		
11		2.1.1 Interview Managers	2 days		
12	▦	2.1.2 Interview Staff	2 days		
13		This task has a 'Start No Earlier Than' constraint on Thu 7/17/03.	2 days		
14		2.3 Feedback Sessions	1 day		

Resources

Until now, we have been looking at planning a project. This chapter introduces organizing a project and working with project resources.

Covers

Chapter Seven

Organizing a Project

Organization is a key area for a project manager. If you are not organized you will quickly lose track of what's happening on your project. The things you will need to organize on your project are the resources that you are going to use in order to complete the tasks and produce the deliverables.

Resources

Resources represent the people and facilities that you will use on your project. As you have seen in the previous chapters, you can produce and schedule a project without assigning resources to it. In fact, if you are going to be doing all the work on a project yourself, you may not even bother to allocate resources (yourself) to the project. On the other hand, if you are going to have other (non-project) work to deal with or if you are going to need other people and things on your project, then you will be able to organize the project much better if you allocate resources.

Resource Information

In Project 2002, you can store lots of information about the resources you will use on your project. Anything from availability (resource calendar) to costs (standard rate, overtime rate, etc.).

Fortunately, setting up resources and their associated information and allocating them to tasks is a very straightforward operation with Project 2002.

Project Stakeholders

The major resources on most projects will be people: the people who will be involved in the project and the people who will do the work. But there are also other people with a vested interest in the outcome of a project: people who will be impacted by it in some way. They could include your management, staff affected by any changes and even your suppliers and customers. The generic term for all these people and groups is "project stakeholders".

It is a good idea to start out by listing all your project stakeholders. You may not need to enter them all as resources but you should certainly keep the list available as you will probably need to think about communicating with them about the project every so often.

So produce a list of your project stakeholders. Ensure you include:

- Your project sponsor or project board (whoever you report to about the project).

- Your project team (the people who will be working with you on completing the tasks).

- Any other people in the business who will be affected by the outcome of the project.

- Customers and suppliers (both internal and external) who will be affected by the outcome of the project.

- Anyone else who could be affected by the project or who could have an impact on it.

When you have identified them all, think about the impact that they could have on your project. If they could have an impact in any way then you need to make sure you communicate what's happening on the project to them.

Remember that no-one likes being kept in the dark: that's where the dreaded FUD (Fear, Uncertainty and Doubt) factor creeps in. After all, you want them all on your side – not against you when the chips are down!

Allocating Resources

People who are assigned to a project are usually assigned on some form of temporary basis. That is, they will be working on your project for a set period of time. They will usually have other jobs and they may even have to keep on doing those other jobs for part of the time while they are also working on your project.

If you have someone allocated to your project for less than 50% of their time, you may find it hard to get them to prioritize project work over their other work.

If you have a person allocated to your project on anything less than a full-time basis you will need to take account of their other work commitments. This will sometimes be on the basis of their being allocated to the project for a certain number of days per week or month. Or it might be on the basis of their being allocated to the project for a percentage of their time (typically, 50% to 80%).

It will be very important to get a firm agreement on any part-time allocations up front, as you may need to fight for key resources at critical times. These are the sort of factors that need to be recorded as part of your project planning document.

The question is: how many days will a person work per week or per month on your project? If you know exactly when they will be available day by day then you can work that way. If not, you need some sort of rule to work to. Something that allows for them to be on vacation, on training courses, off sick, attending company meetings, etc. As a rule of thumb you could use the following:

> There are 52 weeks in a year,
>
> minus 3 weeks' annual leave,
>
> minus 2 weeks' national holidays,
>
> minus 2 weeks' sickness,
>
> minus 2 weeks' training,
>
> minus 1 week for other work-related things.
>
> This leaves 42 weeks at 5 days a week or 210 days at best.

In practice, we have found that it works out at around 190 days on average as there will always be other things that can eat into people's time.

So if people are allocated to your project full-time you will get less than 4 days' work a week from them. If they are not allocated full-time you will get proportionally less. Allocate people and schedule them on this basis (rather than 5 days a week) and you will not get caught out in the resource trap.

The Resource Sheet

If you worked through Chapter 3, you will already have put in some resources. If not, you can add them in now or at the end of this topic (they are all shown on the lower figure).

You can also open it using View>Resource Sheet from the Menu Bar.

Open your project file and click Resource Sheet on the View Bar. The Resource Sheet opens.

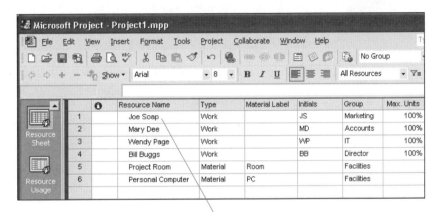

2 Click in the first Resource Name field, press Insert (to create a new resource) and type your project manager's name. Click in Initials and enter them. Click in Group, enter "Proj Mgr" and press Enter. (Don't worry about the other columns for now, just accept the defaults.) Your resources should now look like the following:

The Group field does not have to be used for Department or Group. It can be used for anything you like.

	ⓘ	Resource Name	Type	Material Label	Initials	Group
1		Prudence Project	Work		PP	Proj Mgr
2		Joe Soap	Work		JS	Marketing
3		Mary Dee	Work		MD	Accounts
4		Wendy Page	Work		WP	IT
5		Bill Buggs	Work		BB	Director
6		Project Room	Material	Room		Facilities
7		Personal Computer	Material	PC		Facilities

Once your project is under way you may need to add, amend or even delete resources but it can all be done from this handy Resource Sheet view.

Resource Information

In addition to the Resource Sheet view there is also a Resource Information dialog box.

1 Select one of the Resource Names (Joe Soap) on the Resource Sheet and click the Resource Information button on the Toolbar. The Resource Information dialog box opens.

2 On the General Tab you can input and edit information for this resource. Make the following changes:

Available from:	9/1/2003
Units:	50% (click the down arrow)
Code:	A209
Email:	jsoap@bigco.com
Workgroup:	Email

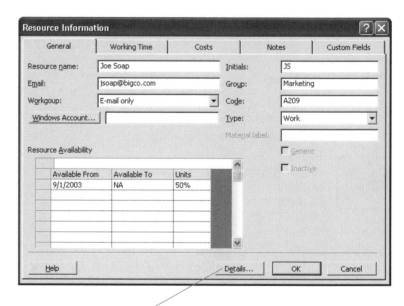

3 Click on the Details button to add more information (such as contact details) and update your email address book. When you are happy with the entry, click OK.

Material Resources

In addition to people, you can also put in other resources or facilities you will be using on your project:

1 Open your project in Resource Sheet view and add in the two additional material resources (resources 8 and 9).

For consumable materials (e.g. paint) the Material Label should specify the units of charge (e.g. liters).

	ⓘ	Resource Name	Type	Material Label	Initials	Group	Max. Units
1		Prudence Project	Work		PP	Proj Mgr	100%
2		Joe Soap	Work		JS	Marketing	0%
3		Mary Dee	Work		MD	Accounts	100%
4		Wendy Page	Work		WP	IT	100%
5		Bill Buggs	Work		BB	Director	100%
6		Project Room	Material	Room		Facilities	
7		Personal Computer	Material	PC		Facilities	
8		Board Room	Material	Room		Facilities	
9		Overhead Projector	Material	OHP		Facilities	

2 Now select one of the material resources and click on the Resource Information button on the Toolbar. Notice on the General tab that all the people-related fields are deselected.

Costs are covered in more detail in the next chapter.

3 Select the Costs tab and the following will be displayed.

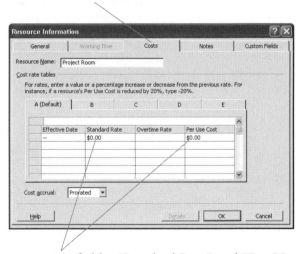

"Overtime Rate" is not used as a cost field on material resources.

There are two cost fields: "Standard Rate" and "Per Use Cost". Standard Rate is used where you will be charged for the duration of the use (e.g. a project room for the duration of the project), while Per Use Cost would apply to occasional use of a facility (e.g. a boardroom for presentations).

Resource Notes

In the same way as you can attach notes to tasks, you can attach notes to a resource:

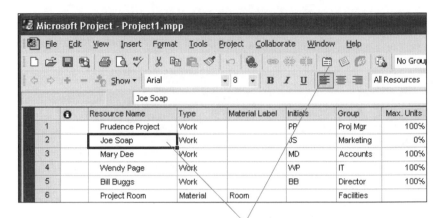

1 On the Resource Sheet select a Resource Name and click the Resource Notes button on the Toolbar. The Resource Information dialog box opens at the Notes tab:

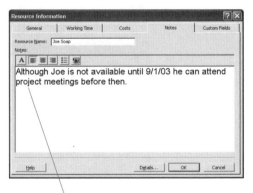

2 Type in your note and click OK. The Resource Sheet now shows a Note in the Information field:

Hold the mouse pointer over the note to have it pop up onscreen.

	❶	Resource Name	Type	Material Label	Initials	Group	Max. Units
1		Prudence Project	Work		PP	Proj Mgr	100%
2	📝	Joe Soap	Work		JS	Marketing	0%
3		Mary Dee	Work		MD	Accounts	100%
4		Wendy Page	Work		WP	IT	100%
5		Bill Buggs	Work		BB	Director	100%
6		Project Room	Material	Room		Facilities	

Notes: 'Although Joe is not available until 9/1/03 he can attend project meetings before then.'

Assigning Resources

The process of allocating a resource to a task is called "assigning".

1 Open your project in Gantt Chart view, select Task 1.1 (Agree Project Objectives) and click the Assign Resources button on the Toolbar.

2 The Assign Resources dialog box appears. Select your project manager's name and click Assign. If you click on the Graphs button you can also see their availability.

 The resource availability graph is a very useful new feature in Project 2002.

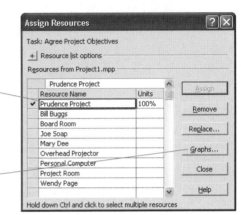

3 Select Task 1.2 (Identify Stakeholders) and assign your project manager to that task as well.

4 Select Task 1.3 (Identify Project Team), select "Bill Buggs", assign him to the task and click Close.

	❶	Task Name	Duration	Jun 30, '03 S M T W T F S	Jul 7, '03 S M T W T
1		⊟ **1 Initiation Stage**	**11 days**		
2		1.1 Agree Project Objectives	1 day	**Prudence Project**	
3	◆	1.2 Identify Stakeholders	1 day	**Prudence Project**	
4		1.3 Identify Project Team	2 days	**Bill Buggs**	
5		1.4 Identify Business Case	2 days		
6		1.5 Analyze the Risks	1 day		
7	📋	1.6 Produce Outline Project Plan	1 day		
8		1.7 Project Approval	0 days		

The Gantt Chart now shows the assignments. Note that these assignments were made at Units of 100% (the whole resource being allocated to the task).

Multiple Resources

So far we have just assigned a single resource to each task (which is in fact the best way of controlling a project). However, sometimes you need to assign two or more people or other resources to a task.

1 Select Task 1.3 (Identify Project Team) and click the Assign Resources button.

2 In the Assign Resources dialog box, click your project manager and click Assign.

	ⓘ	Task Name	Duration	Jun 30, '03	Jul 7, '03	Jul 14, '03
				S M T W T F S	S M T W T F S	S M T W T F
1		⊟ **1 Initiation Stage**	**10 days**			
2		1.1 Agree Project Objectives	1 day	Prudence Project		
3	◆	1.2 Identify Stakeholders	1 day	Prudence Project		
4		1.3 Identify Project Team	1 day	Bill Buggs,Prudence Project		
5		1.4 Identify Business Case	2 days			
6		1.5 Analyze the Risks	1 day			
7	📝	1.6 Produce Outline Project Plan	1 day			
8		1.7 Project Approval	0 days			◆ 7/14

Note that both resources are now allocated to the task and that the duration has reduced to 1 day (2 resources x 1 day duration = 2 days' work). In fact we may still want the task to have a duration of 2 days as the two resources will be working together on it.

This is the standard method of scheduling but there are other options we shall look at in a later topic.

3 In order to keep the duration at 2 days, we can click in the Duration field and change it back to 2 days. A Smart Tag appears asking us to clarify what we intended by the change.

If your schedule didn't do this, check Tools> Level Resources and make sure Manual is selected.

4 Select the first option. The task is rescheduled back to 2 days.

You just increased the duration of this task. Is it because the:
◉ Work required to do this task has increased, so it will take longer
○ Resources will work fewer hours per day, so the task will take longer
None of the above; show me more details

	ⓘ	Task Name	Duration	Jun 30, '03	Jul 7, '03	Jul 14, '03
				S M T W T F S	S M T W T F S	S M T W T F S
1		⊟ **1 Initiation Stage**	**11 days**			
2		1.1 Agree Project Objectives	1 day	Prudence Project		
3	◆	1.2 Identify Stakeholders	1 day	Prudence Project		
4		1.3 Identify Project Team	2 days	Bill Buggs,Prudence Project		
5		1.4 Identify Business Case	2 days			

At the moment, Task 1.4 (Identify Business Case) is scheduled to start one day before the end of Task 1.3 (we put in a 1-day lead time in an earlier topic) but we haven't yet assigned anyone to the task. We'll now see what happens when we do:

You can keep the Assign Resources dialog box open while you are working in Gantt Chart view.

5 Select Task 1.4 (click the Assign Resources button if you had closed it) and assign your project manager to the task.

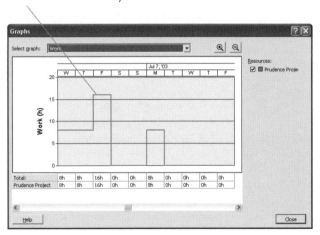

Task Name	Duration
⊟ **1 Initiation Stage**	**11 days**
1.1 Agree Project Objectives	1 day
1.2 Identify Stakeholders	1 day
1.3 Identify Project Team	2 days
1.4 Identify Business Case	2 days
1.5 Analyze the Risks	1 day

Note that although the project manager is already assigned to the previous task (Identify the Project Team) for the first day of Task 1.4, Project 2002 still schedules Task 1.4 to begin on the same day.

6 If you now select the Graph button in the Assign Resources dialog box you will see that the project manager is now overloaded for this day.

We will deal with this situation in the next topic.

We will leave this over-allocation as it stands for the moment but clearly we cannot expect someone to work 16-hour days, even the project manager!

Multiple Tasks

As well as being able to assign multiple resources to a single task, you can also assign resources to multiple tasks:

1 Select Task 1.5 (Analyze the Risks).

2 Hold down Ctrl and select Task 1.6 (Produce Outline Project Plan) and Task 2.1.1 (Interview Managers).

3 Click the Assign Resources button on the Toolbar, select your project manager, click Assign and then Close.

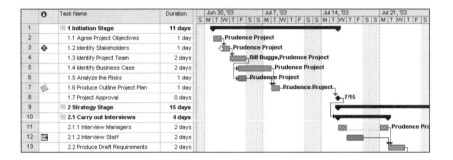

We have now made the situation even worse and what we need to do is level out the work using a process called Resource Leveling.

We look at this leveling process in more detail in a later topic.

4 From the Menu bar select Tools>Level Resources and click the Level Now button. This reschedules the work for us.

One final adjustment we can make is to the split task 2.2.1 (Interview Managers). Now we have rescheduled, it can be brought forward a day.

5 Place your cursor on the second section of the task bar (the cursor changes to 4 arrows) and drag it back to the previous day.

		Task Name	Duration	
		⊟ **2.1 Carry out Interviews**	**4 days**	
		2.1.1 Interview Managers	2 days	
	▥	2.1.2 Interview Staff	2 days	
		2.2 Produce Draft Requirements	2 days	

Project Costs

In this chapter, we look at adding costs to resources and tasks in order to build up the project budget and confirm (or reappraise) the business case for the project.

Covers

Chapter Eight

Project Costs

Be very careful with your preliminary costs or they can end up cast in stone.

One of the first questions a project manager gets asked is "How much is all this going to cost?" and it's usually only moments after being "given" the project in the first place!

No-one can be expected to produce a reliable cost estimate until they have a full grasp of the business requirements. This will only be available a couple of stages into the project. So, anything produced before then should be clearly identified as a preliminary estimate and issued with a corresponding "health warning".

Use Your Experts

Get your Accounts department to run your budgets for you if you can. It's what they're good at.

The people in a business who are best able to produce accurate cost estimates will normally be in a Finance or Accounts section. Using them should not only save the project manager a lot of time, but should also ensure the accuracy of the figures. Some organizations will allocate a finance person to each project as a project accountant.

Costing

This is a guide to developing project costs without a project accountant. Take the internal people work effort (including any change budget) and cost it up (Project 2002 will do this for you). Then add any other internal or external resource or material costs (again Project 2002 will help with this). Then add any recurring costs (the ongoing costs of operating the new product). We will look at each of these in turn:

Internal People Costs

If the business operates on a cost center principle, or charges clients for people's time, it may already have internal charging rates for its people. If not, they can be calculated.

Take the average annual salary for each grade of person working on the project (that way we don't have to know our colleagues' actual salaries!). Double it (to allow for premises and all the other costs of running the business) and divide it by 190 (as explained in "Allocating Resources" on page 96) to get a daily internal cost. It is probably a good idea to check this figure with your finance people to see if they can come up with anything better.

This cost can be used to cost up the time each team member will spend on the project to give the total internal people cost.

External People Costs

External people working on a project will usually be charging for their time in some way. It may be a fixed cost for providing a service or it may be on a daily or hourly rate. Whatever form it takes (and it should be specified in their contract or agreement), it can be used directly as the external people cost.

Other Project Costs

Every project will be different and consequently will be likely to involve different costs. However, these will typically include costs for a project office, furniture, computers, telephones, secretarial services, etc. There may be software costs (such as Project 2002) and there may be a need to include travel and accommodation (which can often be significant on a large or multi-location project) or any other appropriate costs.

Capital Costs

The costs of computers or other equipment, software packages or development, operating systems or database costs will normally be treated as capital (although the business may lease them). The relevant suppliers (or potential suppliers) should provide all of these costs for you. Your business will probably have a standard way of treating capital, depending on whether it leases or purchases and how it depreciates. Whichever way these are treated, they still need to be identified as project costs.

Revenue Operating Costs

This may not be a complete list; there may be other costs that you should account for.

Finally, there are the ongoing or operating costs of the new system, process or product which need to be determined for its expected lifetime. The annual depreciation charge for the capital costs should be determined by the business (see Capital Costs above). The other operating costs will need to be calculated. These could include staff (additional people to operate the new product or procedure), annual maintenance or support costs for hardware (computer or otherwise), annual support or maintenance for software, operating systems, database licenses and any other recurring costs in the project. It is important to recognize all these ongoing costs as they will need to be set against the expected business benefits in appraising the business case (or the justification for the project).

Costs in Project 2002

Having looked at some general considerations about costing in the previous topic, let us now look at how Project 2002 can help. Essentially Project 2002 covers all the (one-off) project costs but not the ongoing operating costs of any solution.

Project 2002 treats costs under two headings: Resource Costs (costs related to the people and material resources you will use on the project) and Fixed Costs (not related to resource usage).

Resource Costs

Once you have identified all the stages, tasks and activities for a project, you will have estimated the work effort required to carry out the project. This should include the appropriate element of change budget (to deal with the unknown) based on where you are in the project. By adding resource costs for all the internal people who will be working on the project, Project 2002 will calculate all the people-related costs for you.

Then you need to identify any external people costs such as consultants, auditors, etc. and feed those in as well.

Finally identify any (non-people) material resource costs if your project is using costed material (such as paint).

Fixed Costs

Once you have the internal and external, people and material resource costs, you then need to identify any internal non-staff costs such as any one-off charges for the use of facilities, rooms, computer usage, etc.

Finally you will need to identify any other external capital or revenue costs such as software package purchase, software development, equipment purchase or lease costs and any other items of external expenditure.

All these costs can be input into Project 2002 as Resource Costs or Fixed Costs on an appropriate task.

We will now work through each of these cost types and use the remaining topics in this chapter to see how they are treated in Project 2002.

Resource Costs

Costs can be applied to resources or tasks. Typically you will use resource costs for people on the project. Costs are normally shown as an hourly rate which can represent their hourly pay rate or salary plus overheads or whatever standards you use for costing in your business.

The easiest way to allocate costs to resources is through the Resource Sheet.

1 Open the Resource Sheet by clicking View>Resource Sheet on the Menu Bar.

If any resources are listed in red they are over-allocated. This is dealt with in a later chapter.

	Resource Name	Type	Material Label	Initials	Group	Max. Units	Std. Rate	Ovt. Rate
1	Prudence Project	Work		PP	Proj Mgr	100%	$20.00/hr	$30.00/hr
2	Joe Soap	Work		JS	Marketing	0%	$25.00/hr	$37.50/hr
3	Mary Dee	Work		MD	Accounts	100%	$15.00/hr	$22.50/hr
4	Wendy Page	Work		WP	IT	100%	$20.00/hr	$30.00/hr
5	Bill Buggs	Work		BB	Director	100%	$40.00/hr	$40.00/hr
6	Project Room	Material	Room		Facilities		$0.00	
7	Personal Computer	Material	PC		Facilities		$0.00	
8	Board Room	Material	Room		Facilities		$0.00	
9	Overhead Projector	Material	OHP		Facilities		$0.00	

2 Enter the applicable standard hourly rates and overtime rates for the resources.

Although the default rate is hourly, you can input a daily or annual rate by adding a "/d" or "/y" after it.

	Resource Name	Type	Material Label	Initials	Group	Max. Units	Std. Rate	Ovt. Rate	Cost/Use
1	Prudence Project	Work		PP	Proj Mgr	100%	$20.00/hr	$30.00/hr	$0.00
2	Joe Soap	Work		JS	Marketing	0%	$25.00/hr	$37.50/hr	$0.00
3	Mary Dee	Work		MD	Accounts	100%	$15.00/hr	$22.50/hr	$0.00
4	Wendy Page	Work		WP	IT	100%	$20.00/hr	$30.00/hr	$0.00
5	Bill Buggs	Work		BB	Director	100%	$40.00/hr	$40.00/hr	$0.00
6	Project Room	Material	Room		Facilities		$0.00		$0.00
7	Personal Computer	Material	PC		Facilities		$0.00		$0.00
8	Board Room	Material	Room		Facilities		$0.00		$0.00
9	Overhead Projector	Material	OHP		Facilities		$0.00		$10.00

3 Where a resource has a Cost Per Use (such as the hire of an overhead projector) enter it in the Cost/Use field.

It is possible for a resource to have both an hourly rate and a Per Use cost, the Per Use cost being charged once each time it is used and the hourly rate charged for the task duration. If this is the case then enter both the Standard rate and the Cost/Use rate.

Fixed Costs

Fixed costs are used where a task has a cost associated with it rather than the cost being associated with the resource. For example, Task 3.3 (Purchase Package) will be the purchase cost of the selected software package.

Project 2002 has adaptive menus, so if you don't see the item you want either click on the expand item (double chevron) or allow your pointer to hover over the menu and it will expand.

I Select the Gantt Chart view then click View>Table: Entry> Cost on the Menu Bar.

The cost columns will be moved into the view replacing the task entry columns in the Gantt Chart view.

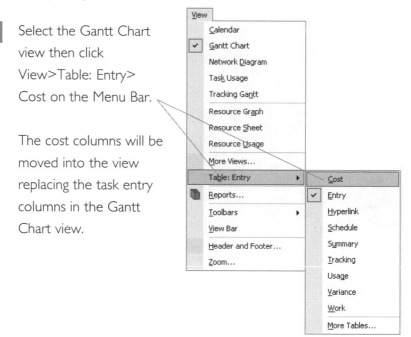

2 Type in the estimated fixed cost for the relevant task (3.3 Purchase Package).

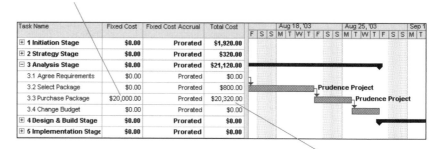

Task Name	Fixed Cost	Fixed Cost Accrual	Total Cost
⊞ 1 Initiation Stage	$0.00	Prorated	$1,920.00
⊞ 2 Strategy Stage	$0.00	Prorated	$320.00
⊟ 3 Analysis Stage	$0.00	Prorated	$21,120.00
3.1 Agree Requirements	$0.00	Prorated	$0.00
3.2 Select Package	$0.00	Prorated	$800.00
3.3 Purchase Package	$20,000.00	Prorated	$20,320.00
3.4 Change Budget	$0.00	Prorated	$0.00
⊞ 4 Design & Build Stage	$0.00	Prorated	$0.00
⊞ 5 Implementation Stage	$0.00	Prorated	$0.00

3 Select tasks 3.1 and 3.2 and assign the project manager to them. Note that the total cost of 3.3 now includes the fixed cost and the resource cost.

Variable Resource Costs

During the life of a project it is quite possible that resource costs could change. For example, someone may receive a promotion and salary increase for doing such a good job on the project. Any cost changes should be entered through the Resource Information dialog box.

1 In Resource Sheet view, select the project manager and click the Resource Information button on the Toolbar.

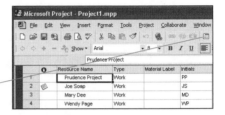

2 Click the Costs tab, click in the next Effective Date field and click the down arrow to get the calendar.

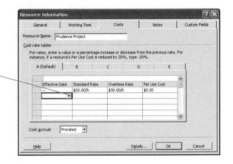

3 Select September 1.

Note: you can also input a percentage figure for an increase (or a minus percentage for a decrease).

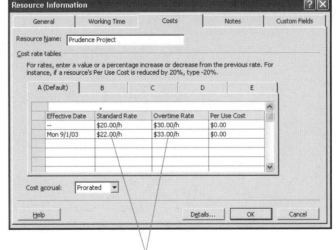

4 Type in the new standard and overtime rates and click OK.

Cost Rate Tables

In addition to being able to change cost rates, Project 2002 will also allow you to set up tables of rates for a resource. This can be useful if you need to use different rates for different types of work for the same person.

The cost rate tables are selected in the Costs tab in the Resource Information dialog box:

1 In Resource Sheet view, double-click Bill Buggs. The Resource Information dialog box opens.

2 Make sure the Costs tab is selected and click Tab B in the Cost rate tables area.

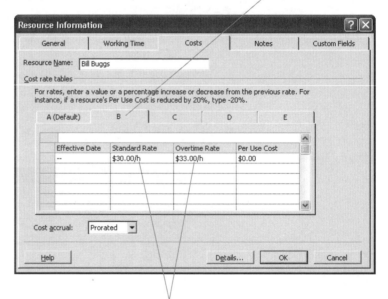

3 Type in the new standard rate "30" and new overtime rate "33".

4 Click Tab A and verify that the default rates have not changed.

5 Click OK to save the new rates table.

Applying Resource Rates

Having set up the new Cost rate table in the previous topic, we can now apply it to any tasks where it is relevant.

Note that the outline numbering is not displayed in Task Usage view.

1 Select View>Task Usage on the Menu Bar and select Task 5 (Identify Business Case).

2 Click on the Assign Resource button and assign Bill Buggs to the task, reducing the duration for the task.

3 Now select Bill Buggs and click the Go To Selected Task button to move the selected task into view.

4 Click the Assignment Information button. The Assignment Information dialog box opens. Select the General tab.

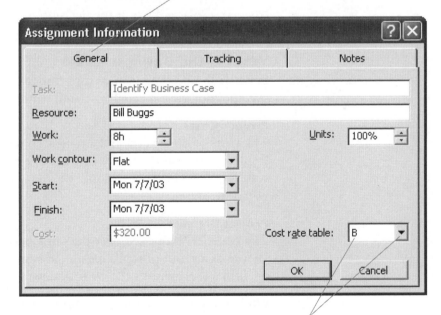

5 Click the Cost rate table down arrow and select Table B.

6 Click OK. The new cost rate table is assigned to the task for Bill Buggs and the costs for the task are recalculated on that basis.

The Business Case

Once you have identified all the costs for the project, it is a good idea to re-examine the business case. The business case is the reason or justification for carrying out the project in the first place and once all the costs are known (or at least estimated), it may be that there is no longer a clear business case. If this is the situation the project should be reconsidered.

Who Owns the Business Case?

The project manager should not be responsible for making or supporting the business case. This is the responsibility of the project sponsor. The project manager's role is to determine the real costs of the project so that the business can make the decision about the viability (or not) of the project.

The costs for a properly planned project will normally start fairly low and gradually build up through the life of the project. Planning should take place at the start of the project so that a reasonable idea of the likely cost is available before too much time and expenditure have taken place. Then if the decision is made to cancel the project, the costs of doing so will still be fairly low.

What is the Business Case?

So what should the business case consist of? Basically, it is just a statement of the expected costs and benefits, defined as:

Project Costs

The costs of the project and any new systems implemented as a result of it over the number of years of expected life of the new systems. The new system could be a computer system or just a new way of working.

Project Benefits

The benefits (expressed over the same period) would represent any savings as a result of replacing an old system, plus any other quantifiable business benefits (e.g. new business revenue).

While the project manager should be responsible for the project costs, the benefits and the decision to go ahead with the project should be defined by the business or the project sponsor on behalf of the business.

Project Calendars

This chapter explains what the various project calendars are, how to create them, set them up for the project and assign and change them for individual resources.

Covers

Chapter Nine

Calendars

Scheduling a project consists of allocating tasks to resources in line with their availability. So, before you can start scheduling you need to know the availability and non-availability of the resources you will be using (e.g. if they are going to be on vacation or on a training course at any time during the project).

Project 2002 uses calendars to determine working and nonworking days, default start time and the working hours in a day.

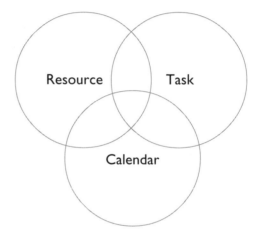

So resources, tasks and availability (the resource calendar) are all interlinked. If any change happens to one of them it can impact on the others and on the project schedule.

There are three types of calendar: base calendars, individual resource calendars and task calendars. Base calendars define the working days and hours for the whole project (or for a group of resources). Resource calendars define the working days and working hours for an individual resource. Task calendars define when a task can or cannot take place.

There are two other base calendars provided: the Night Shift and 24-hour calendars. You can also create your own base calendars.

The standard calendar is the default project base calendar. It defines the working days and hours for the whole project.

When a resource is added to a project, the standard calendar is allocated to that resource as its base calendar. Any changes made to the standard calendar are reflected in the resource calendars that are based on it.

The relationships between the various base calendars, the resource calendars and the project defaults require a little explanation.

If you consider them as three levels, they work like this:

1   Project 2002 uses project defaults to set task duration and in resource allocation. You can change the hours in a day, hours in a week or days in a month that are used for calculation.

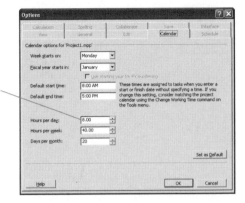

2   Base Calendars are used to define the working days and hours for the project (or a group of resources within it).

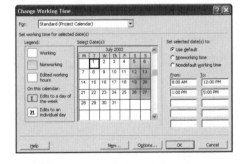

3   Resource Calendars are created for each resource and inherit their base calendar working days and hours. They are used to set variations from the base calendar e.g. annual vacations/meetings. Task calendars are similar to resource calendars but are created for each task that requires one.

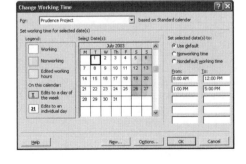

Project Defaults

Project defaults are initially set the same as the standard base calendar. Working time is Monday to Friday, 8:00 AM to 12:00 PM and 1:00 PM to 5:00 PM with no vacations.

Changes to the project defaults will not change base or resource calendars.

Changing the project defaults does not change any of the base calendars or the resource calendars based on them.

Changing the project defaults will change the way that tasks are allocated duration and the way that resources are allocated to them.

If you make any changes to project defaults you must also change the relevant base calendar(s) to keep them in step:

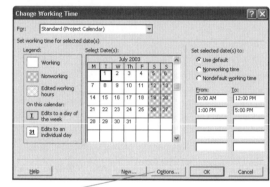

| Click Tools> Change Working Time on the Menu Bar.

You can also click Tools>Options and select the Calendar tab.

2 Click Options. The Options dialog box opens at the Calendar tab.

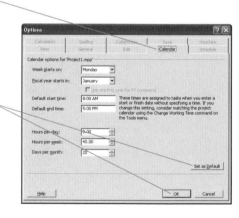

If you are going to make any changes to the working hours, you must do it before you start entering tasks. Once you have entered a task it will be based on the default hours at the time you entered it. If you want to try it out, save your project first, make the changes and see what happens to your schedule.

3 Make any changes and click OK. (Set as Default applies them to all future projects.)

4 If you have made any changes to the days or hours, make sure you make the same changes in your standard/ base calendar and see the BEWARE tip.

Standard Calendar

The standard calendar has a default setting of 8:00 AM to 12:00 PM and 1:00 PM to 5:00 PM for the working hours and Monday to Friday (with no vacations) for the working days.

The first step is to set up the base calendar for your project by making any required changes to the working hours and working days and putting in national holidays or other vacations.

The Change Working Time dialog box is used to implement these changes:

| Click Tools>Change Working Time on the Menu Bar. The Change Working Time dialog box appears:

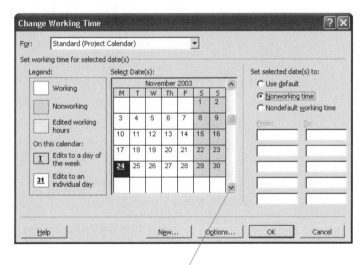

2 Change to November using the scrollbar, select Thursday 27th and click Nonworking time.

3 Change to December, select the 24th, click Nondefault working time and then delete the afternoon working time. You do this by selecting the second From time and deleting it and then the second To time.

If you scroll the Gantt Chart view forward, you will see that these new nonworking days are now gray.

4 Now change December 25th and 26th and January 1st to Nonworking time and click OK.

Creating a New Base Calendar

If none of the available base calendars fit the project requirements, or if you need a base calendar for a group of resources that work different hours, you can create a new one.

A new base calendar can be created from the project calendar defaults or by copying an existing base calendar. This will mean you don't have to redefine vacations, etc.

1 Open the Change Working Time dialog box and click New. The Create New Base Calendar dialog box opens:

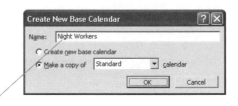

2 Name the new base calendar as "Night Workers". In the Make a copy of... field, select Standard then click OK. The new calendar is selected.

3 Select the day titles for T, W, Th and F by dragging across them and change the working hours to "12:00 AM–5:00 AM" and "9:00 PM–12:00 AM".

If you have people working shifts that span midnight (e.g. 9:00 PM to 05:00 AM), the hours before midnight have to be entered on one day and the hours after midnight on the next day.

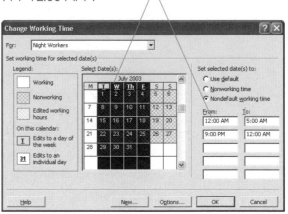

4 Change Monday to "9:00 PM–12:00 AM" and Saturday to "12:00 AM–05:00 AM". Click OK.

Assigning a Calendar

If you create additional base calendars, they can then be assigned to the whole project or to individuals or groups of resources.

The base calendar can be assigned on the Resource Sheet or in the Resource Information dialog box.

If changes have already been made to a resource calendar and a new base calendar is assigned to the resource, the changes will be retained and applied to the new base.

If you do not assign a base calendar, the standard calendar is automatically assigned.

1 In Resource Sheet view double-click on Wendy Page. The Resource Information dialog box opens.

2 Select the Working Time tab. (Note the Base Calendar is currently Standard.)

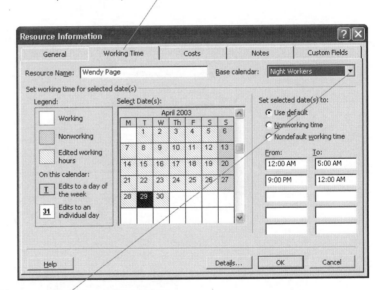

3 Click here, select Night Workers and click OK.

Resource Name	Type	Material Label	Initials	Group	Max. Units	Std. Rate	Ovt. Rate	Cost/Use	Accrue At	Base Calendar
Prudence Project	Work		PP	Proj Mgr	100%	$20.00/hr	$30.00/hr	$0.00	Prorated	Standard
Joe Soap	Work		JS	Marketing	0%	$25.00/hr	$37.50/hr	$0.00	Prorated	Standard
Mary Dee	Work		MD	Accounts	100%	$15.00/hr	$22.50/hr	$0.00	Prorated	Standard
Wendy Page	Work		WP	IT	100%	$20.00/hr	$30.00/hr	$0.00	Prorated	Night Workers
Bill Buggs	Work		BB	Director	100%	$40.00/hr	$40.00/hr	$0.00	Prorated	Standard

4 Wendy Page is now working nights.

Task Calendar

It will sometimes be necessary to define a task that can only take place at a certain time or on certain days. This is possible in Project 2002 by using Task Calendars.

Let's say that you want to make a formal presentation to the company management who have a weekly management meeting on Friday mornings. You need to define the presentation as a task and then give it a task calendar with only Friday mornings as working time. We have a "Report to Management" (Task 2.9) in the project but this has a two-day duration so we will need to split it into subtasks (activities).

1 Open your project in Gantt Chart view, insert two new tasks after Task 2.9 (Report to Management): "Prepare Report" (1.5d) and "Present to Management" (0.5d) and indent them.

Task Name	Duration	Start	28, '03 T W T F S S	Aug 4, '03 M T W T F S
2.6 Evolve Other Recommendations	1 day	Thu 7/31/03		
2.7 Carry out Risk Analysis	2 days	Fri 8/1/03		
2.8 Produce Forward Plan	1 day	Tue 8/5/03		
⊟ **2.9 Report to Management**	**2 days**	**Wed 8/6/03**		
2.9.1 Prepare Report	1.5 days	Wed 8/6/03		
2.9.2 Present to Management	0.5 days	Thu 8/7/03		
⊟ **3 Analysis Stage**	**15 days**	**Fri 8/8/03**		
3.1 Agree Requirements	5 days	Fri 8/8/03		

2 Now create a Management Meeting base calendar by selecting Tools>Change Working Time>New. The Create New Base Calendar dialog box opens:

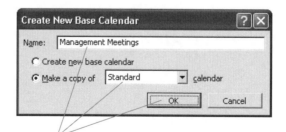

By making a copy of the standard base calendar it will inherit any national holidays and working time.

3 Name the new calendar as "Management Meetings". In the Make a copy of... field, select Standard. Click OK.

4 In the Change Working Time dialog box select Monday to Thursday by dragging across the column headers and make them Nonworking time.

5 Now select Friday, delete the afternoon time (it will change to Nondefault working time) and click OK.

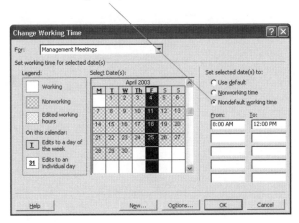

6 Double-click on Task 2.9.2 (Present to Management) to open the Task Information dialog box, select the Advanced tab, select the Management Meetings calendar and click OK.

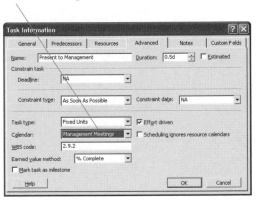

To override the resource calendar for scheduling, select "Scheduling ignores resource calendars".

If a resource with a calendar is now assigned to the task, then the two calendars are combined for the purposes of scheduling when the task can take place.

Changing a Resource Calendar

Each resource is automatically assigned a calendar based on the standard calendar unless a different base calendar is specified. However, while that will include the standard working days and hours for the project, it will not include times that the resource is unavailable at meetings, on vacation or attending a training course.

1 Open your project and select Resource Sheet view.

2 Select "Bill Buggs" and click the Resource Information button on the Toolbar.

You can also double-click on a resource to open the associated Resource Information dialog box.

3 Click the Working Time tab to display his resource calendar.

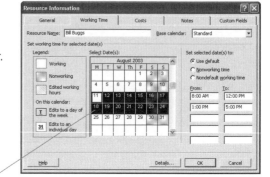

4 Use the scroll bar to move forward to August.

5 Select the middle two weeks.

6 Change the setting in the Set selected date(s) to: section to Nonworking time and click on any day. Buggs will now be on vacation and thus unavailable for the two weeks.

After step 6, the two weeks are shaded to indicate nonworking time and underlined to indicate they are an exception.

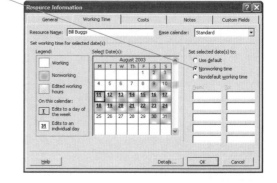

7 Click OK and save your project.

Project Scheduling

This chapter deals with scheduling a project and the effect of different task types on the scheduling process.

Covers

Chapter Ten

Scheduling

The process of scheduling uses the tasks, the resources allocated to them and their calendars to work out when tasks can be started, worked on and completed.

Forward-Scheduling

The default approach to scheduling is to forward-schedule from a start date. You can also backward-schedule from a finish date although there are certain problems that can result from this.

The way that the schedule will be affected when resources, work effort or durations change is also dependent on the scheduling method and task types. The scheduling method can be either effort-driven or not. Tasks can be of fixed-unit, fixed-duration or fixed-work types. The default is fixed-unit, effort-driven but we will look at examples of each of these types.

Effort-Driven Scheduling

Note the following definitions which relate to scheduling:

- *Work is the effort that will be required to complete a task.*
- *Duration is the length of time that it will take to complete a given task.*
- *Units are the resources that will be used to complete a task expressed as a percentage (200% = two resources).*

This is the default scheduling method in Project 2002. In this method the duration of a task is adjusted to fit in with any changes to the resources. If a task is going to require 16 hours' work effort and you allocate two resources to it (at 100%), it will be given a duration of 8 hours or 1 day.

If you then remove one of the resources, the additional day's work will be reallocated to the remaining resource and so the duration will be extended to 2 days.

You can turn effort-driven scheduling off for a specific task or for all new tasks. When effort-driven scheduling is turned off, adding an additional resource to a 2-day duration, fixed-unit task will increase the work effort by 2 days to 4 days, but the duration will remain unchanged (as there are now two people doing it).

Task Types

The task type (fixed-unit, fixed-duration or fixed-work) will determine what will be changed to accommodate any other changes. The basic equation used by Project 2002 is:

Work = Duration x Units

where Work is the work effort required, Duration is how long it will take and Units are resources and their percentage allocation.

Fixed-Unit Tasks

The fixed-unit task is the default task type in Project 2002. If resources are added or removed from a task, the duration is usually affected.

1 Click View>More Views from the Menu Bar, select Task Entry view and click Apply.

2 Select Task 2.3 (Feedback Sessions) and click the Assign Resources button on the Toolbar.

3 Click your project manager and click Assign. Notice in the lower pane that 8 hours' work has been allocated.

4 Now assign Mary Dee to the task as well. (Notice that 4 hours' work is now allocated to each of them and the duration has halved.) Your screen should look something like the following:

Notice the Smart Tag (the diamond icon with an exclamation mark through it) that appears, to give advice and allow you to confirm what you want to do when you add additional resources.

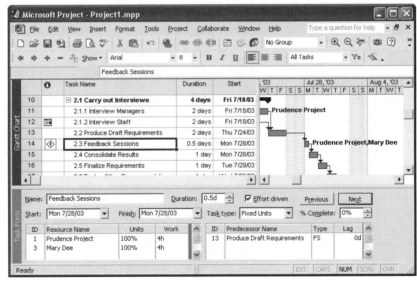

The default task type is fixed-unit which enables you to change the duration by assigning more resources to a task. The other two task types and how they behave are described in the next two topics.

Fixed-Duration Tasks

If a task is a fixed-duration task, then (as the name implies) the duration remains fixed whether resources are added or removed. This has an impact on the way scheduling takes place, depending on whether effort-driven scheduling is being used or not.

Effort-Driven Scheduling

If effort-driven scheduling is being used this means that adding another resource to an existing task will split the work between the two resources. The effort will remain the same, the duration will remain the same so their units will be reduced to 50% to balance.

Non Effort-Driven Scheduling

If effort-driven scheduling is not being used this means that adding another resource to an existing task will double the work. The duration stays the same, the units will be 100%, so the work effort will double.

1   In Task Entry view, select Task 2.6 (Evolve Other Recommendations).

2   In the bottom pane, change the task type to Fixed Duration, deselect Effort Driven and click OK.

With multiple screens, you need to select the top or bottom pane to make it active.

3   Click on task 2.6 again in the top pane (to restore the focus) and click the Allocate Resources button on the Toolbar.

4   Assign your project manager to the task (note at this time nothing has changed on the schedule).

5   Now assign Bill Buggs to the task. The bottom pane should look like the following:

A Smart Tag will appear in the Task Information column to advise on the action taken and offer alternatives.

The duration has stayed the same (1 day), both people are allocated 100%, so the work effort has increased to 2 days (16 hours).

Fixed-Work Tasks

The third task type is fixed-work. A fixed-work task must be effort-driven so only the duration and resource units can be affected.

Adding another resource will reduce the duration while increasing the duration will reduce the resource units.

1 In Task Entry view, in the top pane select Task 2.5 (Finalize Requirements).

2 In the bottom pane change the Task type to Fixed-Work (notice Effort Driven deselects) and click OK.

3 Reselect the task in the top pane and assign your project manager to it (note the work effort is 8 hours).

4 Now assign Bill Buggs to it (note that the work effort is still 8 hours so the duration halves to 0.5 days).

5 Now change the duration back to 1 day on the Task Form (lower pane) and click OK. The resource units are both reduced to 50% so that the work effort remains at 8 hours. Your screen should look something like the following:

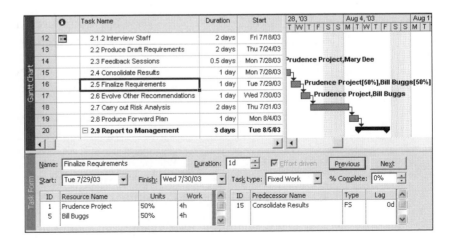

Contouring

When you assign a resource to a task, the total work is spread evenly throughout the duration of the task. This is referred to as a flat contour but there are a number of other contours that you can apply in Project 2002.

Contours can be applied or changed in Task Usage or Resource Usage views. In the former, the resources are grouped by task; in the latter, tasks are grouped by resource. In both cases the right-hand side of the screen displays the work values and is used to contour the work.

Contours are applied using the Assignment Information dialog box. There are eight preset contours available:

Flat	Work hours are distributed evenly through the task duration.
Back Loaded	The hours start low and ramp up towards the end of the task.
Front Loaded	The hours start at 100% at the start of the task and tail off towards the end.
Double Peak	The hours peak twice during the task duration.
Early Peak	The hours peak during the first quarter of the task duration.
Late Peak	The hours peak during the last quarter of the task duration.
Bell	The hours start and finish low and peak in the middle of the task duration.
Turtle	Similar to Bell but the hours start and finish higher (i.e. there is less variation).

Once a contour has been applied to a task, any changes to the task start or finish dates, the resources allocated or the duration will be applied using the contour.

We will now look at applying a contour.

...cont'd

You can drag the heading dividers to increase or decrease the width of a field.

1 Open your project in Resource Usage view and select Analyze the Risks (one of your project manager's tasks).

2 Click the Go To Selected Task button on the Toolbar to bring the task into view and adjust the screen to look like the example at the bottom of this page.

3 Click in the work field for the task and increase the 8 hours to 11 hours. Accept the Smart Tag suggestion and the extra 3 hours are scheduled for the next working day.

4 Click the Assignment Information button on the Toolbar. The Assignment Information dialog box opens:

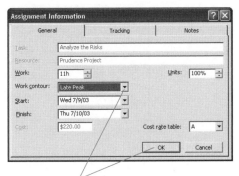

5 Click the Work contour down arrow, change the Work contour to Late Peak and click OK. The work contour changes and a contour indicator is added.

🛈	Resource Name	Work	Details	Jul 7, '03 M	T	W	T	F
	☐ Prudence Project	107 hrs	Work	8h		1.8h	5.95h	5.25h
	Agree Project Objectives	8 hrs	Work					
	Identify Stakeholders	8 hrs	Work					
	Identify Project Team	16 hrs	Work					
	Identify Business Case	8 hrs	Work	8h				
📊	Analyze the Risks	11 hrs	Work			1.8h	5.95h	3.25h
	Produce Outline Project Plan	8 hrs	Work					2h

6 Save your project file and then try applying different contours to see the effect.

Resource Contouring

There is an inconsistency in the way this feature works, which is explained on the facing page.

Project 2002 includes a feature that allows you to contour resource availability. This feature is aimed at situations where an individual is only available to a project part-time, with the percentage of their time available changing from period to period. Alternatively, it would be applicable if a team of people were going to be working on a task or set of tasks and the team were going to have varying numbers of people available over time (perhaps building up the team initially and then releasing them in a phased way).

Applying a resource contour is quite straightforward:

1 Open your project in Resource Sheet view, select your project manager and open the Resource Information dialog box at the General tab.

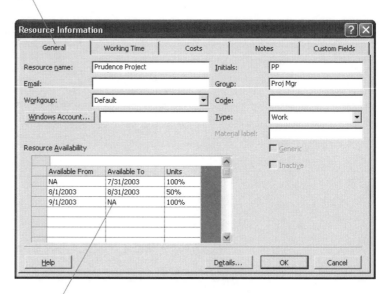

2 Now enter the above availability profile for your project manager and click OK. Your project manager will be highlighted in red and a warning will be placed in the Information column:

	❶	Resource Name	Type	Material Label	Initials	Group
1	⟐	**Prudence Project**	**Work**		**PP**	**Proj Mgr**
2		This resource should be leveled based on a Day by Day setting.			JS	Marketing
3					MD	Accounts

3   Now change to Gantt Chart view and select Task 2.7 (Carry out Risk Analysis) and click on the Go To Selected Task button to bring the Task bar into view.

4   Assign the task to your project manager and note what happens:

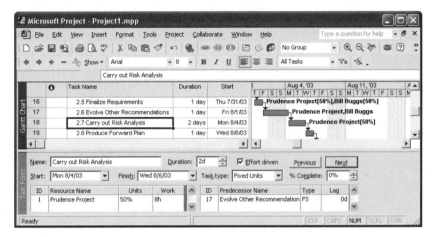

The project manager has been correctly allocated at 50% but the duration has stayed at 2 days, which is only 8 hours' work effort!

5   Although it is a fixed-unit task, it has behaved like a fixed duration task as it should have increased to 4 days. To correct this, increase the Duration in the Task Form (lower pane) to 4 days and the task is correctly assigned (Work effort = 16 hours, Unit availability = 50% and Duration = 4 days):

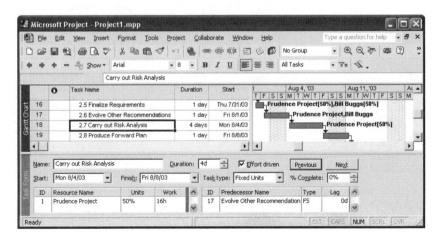

If and when you come to use resource contouring, bear this issue (and how to fix it) in mind.

Backward Scheduling

The default method of scheduling is forward scheduling from the project start date. This is what we have been using so far. However, there are times when you have to complete a project by a certain date in the future. By scheduling backwards from a finish date, you can see when a project has to start. However, there is a right and a wrong way to go about it in Project 2002.

The Right Way

It is good practice to save your project before making any major changes to it. Just in case!

If you are going to use backward scheduling, then use it right from the start. When you first create your project set it to schedule from the required completion date:

1. Create a new project and select Project>Project Information from the Menu bar. Select "Schedule from: Project Finish Date", select the date you want the project to finish and click OK.

Then as you start to input your tasks and allocate resources, Project 2002 will correctly backward-schedule your project.

But what if you start off with forward scheduling and then decide you need to switch to backward scheduling?

The Wrong Way

Project 2002 will allow you to change from forward to backward scheduling but things are not always what they seem. If you want to try this, please save your project file first!

1. Open your project in Gantt Chart view, select Show Outline Level 1 (to hide all subtasks) and zoom out to get the whole project into view.

If you do have to change to backward scheduling, it is usually easier to start again with a new project file as in "The Right Way" above.

2. Select Project>Project Information from the Menu bar, change Schedule from: to Project Finish Date, select your required finish date and click OK.

3. Accept any warnings and carry on until the project is rescheduled. Sometimes this works and sometimes it doesn't, so close the project without saving it or save it with a different name.

Conflicts and Constraints

This chapter deals with resource conflicts, manual and automatic leveling and the use of task constraints. It also introduces setting a baseline and saving interim plans.

Covers

Chapter Eleven

Resource Conflicts

As you begin to assign resources to tasks and then make subsequent changes to tasks/schedules, you'll begin to get resource conflicts.

A resource conflict is where a resource is scheduled to perform more work than it can carry out in the time available. Project 2002 flags these conflicts for you by highlighting the relevant resource information in red and displaying a leveling indicator. Once these conflicts are identified the schedule needs to be examined and a decision made on how to resolve the conflict.

You can resolve these conflicts manually using Project 2002 scheduling or you can let Project 2002 automatically adjust the schedule by changing resources or task assignments for you. We will start by creating a resource conflict:

1   Open your project in Gantt Chart view and select Task 1.6 (Produce Outline Project Plan). Make a note of the date it is currently scheduled for (July 11th in our example).

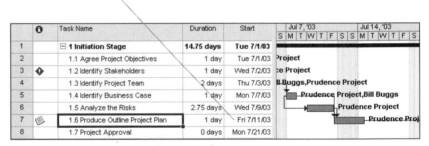

2   Open the Task Information dialog box, select the Advanced tab, change the Constraint type to Finish No later Than, set the Constraint date to one day earlier than it currently is scheduled for and click OK.

3   In the Planning Wizard warning select the third option (Continue to set the constraint) and click OK. In the scheduling conflict warning, select Continue, allow the scheduling conflict and click OK. We now have a resource conflict between Task 1.5 (Analyze the Risks) and Task 1.6 (Produce Outline Project Plan).

Effectively we are asking our project manager to carry out two tasks at once, as can be seen from the following:

ⓘ	Task Name	Duration	Start	Jul 7, '03 S M T W T F S	Jul 14, '03 S M T W T F S S
	1.4 Identify Business Case	1 day	Mon 7/7/03	▭ Prudence Project,Bill Buggs	
	1.5 Analyze the Risks	2.75 days	Wed 7/9/03	▭ Prudence Project	
▣ ◫	1.6 Produce Outline Project Plan	1 day	Thu 7/10/03	▭ Prudence Project	
	1.7 Project Approval	0 days	Thu 7/17/03	◆ 7/17	

4 Change to Resource Sheet view and notice that any over-allocated resources are highlighted in red and have a warning symbol in the Information column.

	ⓘ	Resource Name	Type	Material Label	Initials	Group	Max. Units
1	◇⊹	**Prudence Project**	**Work**		**PP**	**Proj Mgr**	**100%**
2	◪ ◇ This resource should be leveled based			JS	Marketing	0%
3	on a Day by Day setting.			MD	Accounts	100%
4		Wendy Page	Work		WP	IT	100%
5		Bill Buggs	Work		BB	Director	100%
6		Project Room	Material	Room		Facilities	
7		Personal Computer	Material	PC		Facilities	
8		Board Room	Material	Room		Facilities	
9		Overhead Projector	Material	OHP		Facilities	

5 From the Menu bar select View>Toolbars>Resource Management to open the Resource Management Toolbar.

6 Click the Resource Allocation view button on the Resource Management Toolbar.

7 Click the Go To Next Overallocation button (third from the left).

We will look at both leveling approaches in the next two topics.

The overallocation details are displayed in the view. The top pane shows the details of the problem: the project manager is going to have to work 13.95 hours in a single day. The lower pane shows a view of the Gantt Chart at the same level of detail. You can use the Go To Next Overallocation button to view any further overallocations. You can then make manual adjustments or let Project level the work for you.

Resource Leveling

Resource conflicts can be resolved manually or automatically. The process used by Project 2002 to resolve conflicts is termed "resource leveling".

The Resource Leveling dialog box is used to carry out leveling adjustments.

Always save your project before leveling. Then if anything goes wrong you can get back to where you were.

I	In Resource Allocation view, click Project>Project Information on the Menu bar. Note the current project finish date and click Cancel.

2	Select the lower (Leveling Gantt) pane so it is active.

3	Click Tools>Level Resources on the Menu bar.

You can select Automatic leveling to let Project sort out leveling for you automatically as you enter tasks and allocate resources.

4	Check Manual and the other options should be as shown.

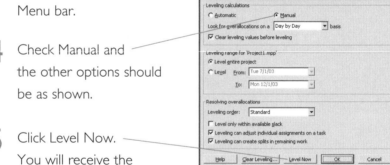

5	Click Level Now. You will receive the following warning:

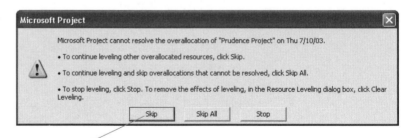

6	Click Skip to continue leveling. When it is finished, note the project finish date. It should have leveled without any slippage but in this case it has slipped one week - we'll soon see why.

...cont'd

Resource Leveling Issues

This turns out to be another issue with Project. When we allocated our project manager to this task (on page 110), she was allocated at 100% so the 5 days' work was scheduled as 5 days' duration.

When we reduced the project manager's availability to 50% for August (on page 132), it did not change this schedule. But now that we have performed resource leveling, Project has failed to cope. It has scheduled the first half-a-day (using the available 50%) but then split the task until September (when 100% is available again). This is clearly not right but we can fix it.

1 In Gantt Chart view, select task 3.2 (Select Package) and click on the Go To Selected Task button to bring it into view.

Task Name	Duration	Start
3.1 Agree Requirements	5 days	Fri 8/15/03
3.2 Select Package	5 days	Fri 8/22/03
3.3 Purchase Package	2 days	Fri 9/5/03
3.4 Change Budget	3 days	Tue 9/9/03

2 Open the Assign Resources dialog box, select your project manager and click the Remove button. If you receive a scheduling conflict warning, accept it. The task is brought back to 5 days' duration.

3 Now assign your project manager to the task again. The schedule remains unaltered at 5 days' duration and the project manager is assigned at 50% availability:

Task Name	Duration	Start
3.1 Agree Requirements	5 days	Fri 8/15/03
3.2 Select Package	5 days	Fri 8/22/03
3.3 Purchase Package	2 days	Fri 8/29/03
3.4 Change Budget	3 days	Tue 9/2/03

This assumes the task will take 5 days even with the project manager at 50% availability. If it would take 10 days now, then it could be adjusted in the same way as we adjusted Task 2.7 (Carry out Risk Analysis) in "Resource Contouring" on pages 132–133.

Manual Adjustments

In addition to using automatic resource leveling you also have to resolve some conflicts manually. You sometimes need to make manual adjustments to stop Project 2002 from automatically extending the schedule if it is unacceptable or where Project 2002 was unable to resolve a conflict (as in the previous topic).

To manually resolve a conflict you will need to take steps such as the following:

- Allocating more resources to a task.

- Rescheduling or splitting a task.

- Adding overtime working.

- Reallocating tasks to a different resource.

1 In Gantt Chart view assign your project manager to all unallocated tasks (if you receive any warnings, accept them).

2 Click the Resource Allocation view button and then the Go To Next Overallocation button on the Resource Management toolbar. Task 6 (Analyze the Risks) and task 7 (Produce Outline Plan) are causing an overallocation.

The Assign Resources button is exactly the same as the version on the Standard Toolbar.

3 In the lower pane (Gantt Chart), select Task 6 (Analyze the Risks) and click the Assign Resources button on the Resource Management Toolbar.

4 Select your project manager and click Replace (to replace her), select Mary Dee, click OK and click Close.

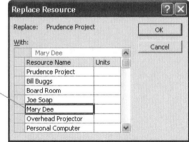

5 Click the Go To Next Over Allocation button. Tasks 11 and 12 are causing it. By reallocating Task 12 to a different resource (Mary Dee again) you can resolve the conflict.

...cont'd

As we have just seen, we can resolve any overallocation by reallocating tasks to a different resource. But there are a number of other manual adjustments we can make:

Allocating More Resources
We can add additional resources to a task using the Assign Resources button (see "Fixed-Unit Tasks" on page 127).

Rescheduling a Task
We can reschedule one or both of the tasks that is causing the overallocation to another time when the required resource is available by moving the task to a new time (see "Moving Linked Tasks" on page 92).

For more on splitting a task, see page 91.

Splitting a Task
We can split a task using the Split Task button.

Overtime Working
Or we can introduce overtime working. Let's say that we need to have Task 4.1 (Design) completed earlier and our project manager has agreed to work 2 hours' overtime per day on this task.

1 Check the dates that the task is being carried out then select Tools>Change Working Time. Select the calendar for your project manager.

2 Select the month when the task is to be carried out.

3 Select the appropriate days, click Nondefault working time, change the end time to 7.00 PM and click OK.

The task still shows a duration of 10 days (which is 80 hours) but it is being completed in 8 calendar days (8 x 10 hours = 80 hours) so finishing two days before.

Task Constraints

When tasks are first entered into a project, they have the project start date as their start date (unless the project is backwards scheduled, in which case they have the project finish date as their finish date). As they are linked and have resources assigned to them, they will be scheduled depending on their dependencies and resource availability and be given their own start and finish dates.

Sometimes these allocated start and finish dates are not viable in the real world and a start or finish date has to be imposed. When this happens it is called setting a "task constraint".

Task constraints are set in the form of start or finish on (or near) a particular date, no earlier or later than a particular date, or as soon or as late as possible. The default constraint which is applied to all tasks on a forward scheduled project is As Soon As Possible. For a backward scheduled project, the default constraint is As Late As Possible.

Too many constraints will make it difficult to resolve schedule conflicts.

Constraints can also be flexible or inflexible. A flexible constraint is one where the project finish date can be moved by the task. An inflexible constraint is one where the project finish date cannot be moved by the task. The following table lists the constraint types and whether they are flexible:

Constraint	Flexible for
As Soon As Possible	All projects
As Late As Possible	All projects
Finish No Earlier Than	Forward-scheduled projects
Start No Earlier Than	Forward-scheduled projects
Finish No Later Than	Backward-scheduled projects
Start No Later Than	Backward-scheduled projects

The first two constraints do not use a date, while all the others have a date associated with them. The date is the earliest or latest date that the task can start or finish (as appropriate to the constraint).

Applying Constraints

The usual reason for applying a constraint to a task is that some internal or external factor means that it can only happen at a particular time.

For example, if you did not want to start using a new accounting package until the start of the new year (January 1st), you might well want to set a Start No Earlier Than constraint:

1 In Gantt Chart view select Task 5.2 (Convert to New Package) and click the Go To Selected Task button.

2 Double-click the task – the Task Information dialog opens.

3 Select the General tab and note the current start and finish dates for the task.

4 Click the Advanced tab, select the Start No Earlier Than constraint and select the date as January 1, 2004.

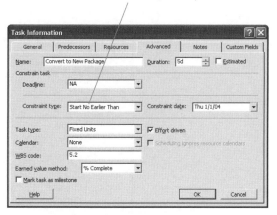

5 Click OK and accept any warnings. The constraint is set, the schedule adjusted and an indicator added:

We set January 1st as a holiday, so the task is not scheduled to start until the 2nd.

Constraint Conflicts

If you set a constraint that causes a conflict, the Planning Wizard appears, to warn you of the problem and offer suggestions where appropriate.

1 Save your project, then in Gantt Chart view double-click on Task 2.9.2 (Present to Management). The Task Information dialog box opens.

2 Click the General tab and note the current finish date.

3 Click the Advanced tab and select Must Finish On as the constraint.

4 Select the previous Friday's date (8/8/03) and click OK. The Planning Wizard dialog box opens, warning you of the scheduling conflict that could occur if you go ahead and set the constraint:

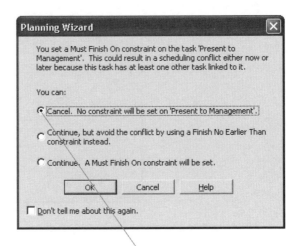

Do not do this unless you have saved your project first. Close your project without saving it (or save it under a different name) afterwards.

5 Normally, you should cancel the constraint. If you have saved your project file, select the third option to Continue and click OK. You will get a further scheduling conflict warning. If you still continue, the schedule will be updated but Task 2.9.2 now needs to start before Task 2.9.1 is completed!

Viewing Constraints

When a task has a constraint applied in Project 2002, there will be an indicator present. If you pause your cursor over it a pop-up will display details of the constraint. In addition, a flexible constraint will have a blue dot and an inflexible constraint a red dot in the constraint symbol.

You can also see constraints via the Constraints Date Table:

1 Open your project in Gantt Chart view and pause your cursor over the indicator on Task 1.6 (Produce Outline Project Plan). It is an inflexible constraint (indicated by the red dot). The constraint details appear in a pop-up box (along with any notes).

2 Do the same for Task 5.2 (Convert to New Package) which has a blue dot (flexible constraint).

4 Select View>Table>More Tables from the Menu bar. The More Tables dialog box appears.

5 Select Constraint Dates and click Apply. The Constraint Dates Table is displayed:

	Task Name	Duration	Constraint Type	Constraint Date
1	⊟ 1 Initiation Stage	13 days	As Soon As Possible	NA
2	1.1 Agree Project Objectives	1 day	As Soon As Possible	NA
3	1.2 Identify Stakeholders	1 day	As Soon As Possible	NA
4	1.3 Identify Project Team	2 days	As Soon As Possible	NA
5	1.4 Identify Business Case	1 day	As Soon As Possible	NA
6	1.5 Analyze the Risks	2.75 days	As Soon As Possible	NA
7	1.6 Produce Outline Project Plan	1 day	Finish No Later Than	Thu 7/10/03
8	1.7 Project Approval	0 days	As Soon As Possible	NA
9	⊞ 2 Strategy Stage	20.5 days	As Soon As Possible	NA
23	⊞ 3 Analysis Stage	15 days	As Soon As Possible	NA
28	⊞ 4 Design & Build Stage	37.25 days	As Soon As Possible	NA
32	⊟ 5 Implementation Stage	57.75 days	As Soon As Possible	NA
33	5.1 Train Users	5 days	As Soon As Possible	NA
34	5.2 Convert to New Package	5 days	Start No Earlier Than	Thu 1/1/04
35	5.3 Change Budget	10 days	As Soon As Possible	NA

Select View> Table>Entry to get back to the standard Gantt Chart view.

Setting a Baseline

Once you have created your project plan, allocated resources, resolved any conflicts and are happy with the project schedule, you are ready to set a baseline.

A baseline represents a record of a set point in time where you have agreed and fixed your project plan. Project 2002 can now hold up to eleven baselines for a project, named Baseline (for the first one) and then Baseline 1 through to 10.

The first baseline you set should contain the original plan only; subsequent baselines will contain the current plan with any actual data up to that point.

When you set a baseline the dates, times and other data are recorded for all tasks.

1 Open your project in Gantt Chart view.

2 Select Tools>Tracking>Save Baseline from the Menu bar.

Baselines 1–10 can also be selected in the Save Baseline dialog. Additionally, previously saved baselines can be updated by saving them again.

3 Select the Save baseline and Entire project options.

4 Click OK. The project is now baselined.

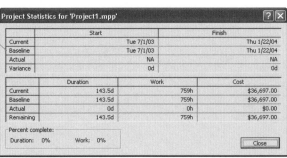

5 Select Project>Project Information and click Statistics on the dialog box. This shows the project's current, baseline and actual details.

	Start	Finish
Current	Tue 7/1/03	Thu 1/22/04
Baseline	Tue 7/1/03	Thu 1/22/04
Actual	NA	NA
Variance	0d	0d

	Duration	Work	Cost
Current	143.5d	759h	$36,697.00
Baseline	143.5d	759h	$36,697.00
Actual	0d	0h	$0.00
Remaining	143.5d	759h	$36,697.00

Percent complete:
Duration: 0%   Work: 0%

Interim Plans

As well as setting up to eleven baselines (which should be retained throughout the project) you can also create up to ten interim plans during the project.

You may wish to create a new baseline at the end of each project stage to reflect any changes to the project that have been agreed during that stage. But you may also wish to use interim plans to track more detailed changes to the project.

While a baseline saves a lot of information about a project, an interim plan just saves details of the current task start/end dates.

1 Select Tools>Tracking>Save Baseline from the Menu bar.

2 Select Save interim plan. In Copy, select Start/Finish. In Into, select Start1/Finish1. In For, select Entire project. Click OK.

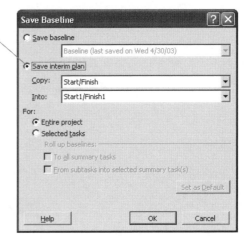

3 As the project progresses you can copy into Start2/Finish2 and so on.

4 You can also update any existing interim plans by copying over a previous interim plan in Copy Into.

5 If you want to save interim plans for one or more tasks rather than the whole project, select the required tasks before selecting Tools>Tracking>Save Baseline (as in Step 1 above).

At the end of the project or stage, you will be able to look back at the interim plans as well as the original baseline and any further baselines as part of your project or stage review.

Clearing a Baseline

In earlier versions of Microsoft Project there used to be no easy method for clearing the baseline data for a project. This was particularly true for time-based data. It is now possible to clear any of the baselines or interim plan data for the whole project or selected tasks.

If you have not already done so, save your project file before clearing the baseline.

1   From the Menu bar select Tools>Tracking>Clear Baseline. The Clear Baseline dialog box opens:

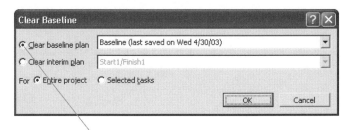

2   Select Clear baseline plan, select Entire project and click OK. The baseline is removed (select Project>Project Information and click Statistics to confirm the baseline data has gone).

3   In Gantt Chart view select Tasks 5.1 to 5.3 (the Implementation Stage) and reopen the Clear Baseline dialog (as in Step 1).

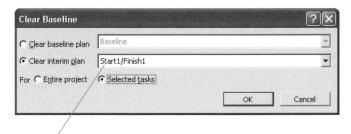

Don't save your project file after clearing the baseline (or save it using a different file name) if you are going to be working through further topics.

4   Select Start1/Finish1 in Clear interim plan. Select Selected tasks (as shown above) and click OK. The interim plan is removed for the selected tasks. We will see more of this in a later topic.

Viewing Data

Project 2002 holds a vast amount of information on your project but you cannot see it all at the same time. It provides many options for selecting and viewing just the data you want at any particular time. This chapter covers the different ways of viewing, grouping, filtering and sorting data and how to tailor views to your specific project requirements.

Covers

Chapter Twelve

Views

In Project 2002, views are the way that data is displayed for you to view and work on. They can be placed into two main categories: task views and resource views. There are 18 task views and 6 resource views. You normally use task views when working with task information and resource views when working with resource information. The views can be further divided into sheets, charts, graphs and forms.

Sheets

Sheets display information in rows and columns (similar to a spreadsheet) with each task or resource being a row (horizontal) and each field in the task or resource being a column (vertical).

Charts and Graphs

Charts display graphical information in chart form, typical examples being the Gantt Chart and Network Diagram views. Graphs are used to display statistical information graphically in views such as Resource Graph and Calendar.

Forms

Forms are used for the display and entry of detailed information on a task or resource.

Some views (such as Calendar) are simple, single views and some are compound views (such as Gantt Chart which shows a sheet on the left and a chart on the right). You can also display a single view or two views (one above the other) as below:

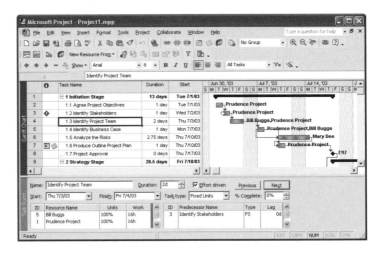

Tables

When working in a sheet view there are a number of preset tables that can be used (applied) to access different types of information on tasks or resources. There are 17 task tables that can be applied to task views and 10 resource tables applicable to resource views.

If the view you have currently selected is not displaying quite the right information you can apply a different table to change the view. The tasks or resources displayed remain the same but you will see different bits of information for them.

1 Open your project in Gantt Chart view and select View>Table: Cost from the Toolbar. The Cost Table displays:

You can see several more cost fields (e.g. Baseline, Variance and Actual) by moving the vertical divider.

	Task Name	Fixed Cost	Fixed Cost Accrual	Total Cost	Jun 30, '03 M T W T F S S	Jul 7, '03 M T W T F S
1	☐ 1 Initiation Stage	$0.00	Prorated	$2,005.00		
2	1.1 Agree Project Objectivi	$0.00	Prorated	$160.00	Prudence Project	
3	1.2 Identify Stakeholders	$0.00	Prorated	$160.00	Prudence Project	
4	1.3 Identify Project Team	$0.00	Prorated	$960.00		Bill Buggs,Prudence P
5	1.4 Identify Business Case	$0.00	Prorated	$400.00		Prudence Pro
6	1.5 Analyze the Risks	$0.00	Prorated	$165.00		
7	1.6 Produce Outline Projec	$0.00	Prorated	$160.00		Prud
8	1.7 Project Approval	$0.00	Prorated	$0.00		

2 Switch to Task Usage view and select View>Table: Work from the Toolbar. The Work Table displays:

Task Name	Work	Baseline	Variance	Actual	Details	Jun 30, '03 M	T	W	T
☐ Initiation Stage	83 hrs	0 hrs	83 hrs	0 hrs	Work		8h	8h	16h
☐ Agree Project Objectives	8 hrs	0 hrs	8 hrs	0 hrs	Work		8h		
Prudence Project	*8 hrs*	*0 hrs*	*8 hrs*	*0 hrs*	Work		8h		
☐ Identify Stakeholders	8 hrs	0 hrs	8 hrs	0 hrs	Work			8h	
Prudence Project	*8 hrs*	*0 hrs*	*8 hrs*	*0 hrs*	Work			8h	
☐ Identify Project Team	32 hrs	0 hrs	32 hrs	0 hrs	Work				16h
Prudence Project	*16 hrs*	*0 hrs*	*16 hrs*	*0 hrs*	Work				8h
Bill Buggs	*16 hrs*	*0 hrs*	*16 hrs*	*0 hrs*	Work				8h
☐ Identify Business Case	16 hrs	0 hrs	16 hrs	0 hrs	Work				
Prudence Project	*8 hrs*	*0 hrs*	*8 hrs*	*0 hrs*	Work				
Bill Buggs	*8 hrs*	*0 hrs*	*8 hrs*	*0 hrs*	Work				

3 Try applying the various different tables to the views that you use to see what is available. When you have finished apply the default (Entry) tables again.

Grouping

Grouping allows you to view your project tasks or resources grouped by any defined criteria. This can be applied to most task and resource views but not Calendar, Network Diagram, Relationship Diagram, Resource Graph and Form views. Each view has various standard groups to select from.

1 Open your project in Resource Sheet view and click the down arrow to the right of the Group By field.

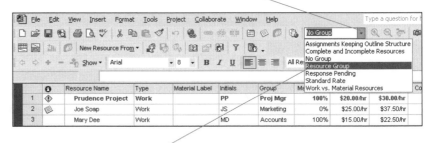

2 Select Resource Group and the Resource Sheet is rearranged by Resource within Group:

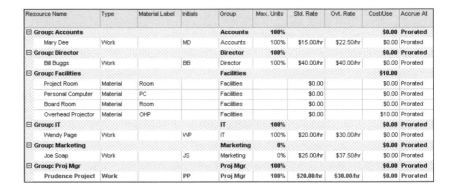

3 Try selecting the other Group By options in the drop-down list and finally re-select No Groups to return to the standard view.

4 Now change to Gantt Chart view, select Show>Outline Level 1, then select Group By>Constraint Type. Note that all non-summary tasks are now displayed but no summary tasks; in their place, the Constraint types are displayed.

The As Soon As Possible tasks have been hidden in this illustration as there are so many of them.

ⓘ	Task Name	Duration	Start	Finish	03 W T F S	Jul 14, '03 S M T W T F S
	⊞ Constraint Type: As Soon As Pos	143.5 days	Tue 7/1/03	Thu 1/22/04		
	⊟ Constraint Type: Finish No Later	1 day	Thu 7/10/03	Thu 7/10/03		
🖬⊘	1.6 Produce Outline Project Plan	1 day	Thu 7/10/03	Thu 7/10/03	▬ Prudence Project	
	⊟ Constraint Type: Start No Earlier	120.5 days	Fri 7/18/03	Thu 1/8/04		
🖬	2.1.2 Interview Staff	2 days	Fri 7/18/03	Mon 7/21/03		▬
🖬	5.2 Convert to New Package	5 days	Fri 1/2/04	Thu 1/8/04		

This is a useful view to see which constraints you have set on which tasks. The group "summary tasks" behave in the same way as the normal summary tasks and the view can be expanded and contracted by clicking the small plus or minus sign beside the group name.

The other useful feature is that Project 2002 rolls up totals by these groupings for you, useful for monitoring costs and work effort.

5 Select Gantt Chart view and then select Group By>Critical. The new grouping is applied to the Gantt Chart.

6 Now select View>Table: Work from the Menu bar. The rolled up work effort totals are displayed on the Critical and non-critical summary lines:

Task Name	Work	Baseline	Variance	Jun 30, '03 S M T W T F S	Jul 7, '03 S M T W T F S
⊟ Critical: Yes	203 hrs	0 hrs	203 hrs		
1.1 Agree Project Objectives	8 hrs	0 hrs	8 hrs	▬Prudence Project	
1.2 Identify Stakeholders	8 hrs	0 hrs	8 hrs	▬Prudence Project	
1.3 Identify Project Team	32 hrs	0 hrs	32 hrs	▬Bill Buggs,Prudence P	
1.4 Identify Business Case	16 hrs	0 hrs	16 hrs	▬Prudence Pro	
1.5 Analyze the Risks	11 hrs	0 hrs	11 hrs		
1.6 Produce Outline Project Plan	8 hrs	0 hrs	8 hrs		▬ Prud
5.2 Convert to New Package	40 hrs	0 hrs	40 hrs		
5.3 Change Budget	80 hrs	0 hrs	80 hrs		

You probably won't want to use most of the Group By options but it is worth knowing what is available.

7 Now try out the other Group By options on the Gantt Chart view and finally try the options on other views.

Customized Groups

While there are a good number of standard Group By options built into the standard views, you may also wish to define your own custom groups. You can define these based on one or more criteria. Finally the color, pattern and font of the group bands can be customized along with the sequence of sorting:

1 Open your project in Gantt Chart view and select Project> Group By>Customize Group By from the Menu bar. The Customize Group By dialog box opens.

2 Select the first Field Name field and select Resource Names from the list. Select the second Field Name field and select Critical from the list. Click OK to create the custom group.

3 The dialog can also be used to define the font, background and pattern of the group summary tasks. Numerical fields can also be grouped by using the Define Group Intervals button:

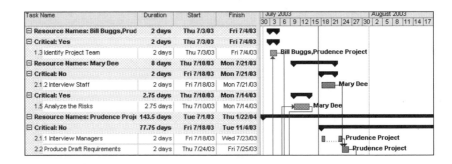

Fiscal Year

Project 2002 has introduced a third timescale (top). The old major timescale is now middle while the old minor is now bottom.

Project 2002 allows you to set the use of the fiscal year for the top, middle or bottom tier timescales. This feature is useful where the business (fiscal) year may be different from the calendar year.

1 Open your project in Gantt Chart view and select Tools>Change Working Time>Options from the Menu bar. The Options dialog box opens:

2 Change Fiscal year starts in to April, select Use starting year for FY numbering and click OK. Click OK again to close the Change Working Time dialog box.

You can also get the Timescale dialog box by double-clicking on the timescale on the Gantt Chart.

3 Select Format>Timescale from the Menu bar.

4 Set the middle tier to Years and deselect Use fiscal year. Set the bottom tier to Quarters and select Use fiscal year. Click OK. The major timescale now displays calendar years and the minor scale displays fiscal quarters (as shown in Preview above).

Filters

In addition to its other selection capabilities, Project 2002 also allows you to filter and sort data before viewing (or printing). Filtering allows you to select just the information that you wish to be displayed.

Predefined Filters

There are a number of predefined filters that you can use to select things such as late tasks, tasks in progress, work that is over budget, and so on. Project 2002 actually contains 32 predefined task filters and 23 predefined resource filters. In addition, you can also create your own custom filters to meet your project's requirements.

Filters can be used to focus on specific tasks in your project or on specific resources in the project. When you apply a filter, only the tasks or resources that meet the filter criteria are displayed. All other tasks and resources are hidden while you are using a filter.

Applying filters to your project does not change the data in any way, it just changes the way you are viewing it.

AutoFilter

Project 2002 contains an AutoFilter feature which gives you a quick way of finding particular information in a field. When it's turned on, each column heading has an arrow on the right-hand side which can be used to apply a filter to the information in the column. You can apply filters to as many columns as you like and once a filter is applied to a column, the column title turns blue.

Interactive Filters

As well as specific filters you can apply interactive filters which display a dialog box during the filtering process. You then provide the information to the dialog box to allow it to complete the filtering process.

Custom Filters

If none of the predefined filters meet your requirements you can create a custom filter that exactly matches your needs. You can copy an existing filter and then edit it to meet your needs or you can create a completely new filter. The Filter Definition dialog box provides shortcuts to simplify this process.

AutoFilter

When AutoFilter is turned on you can apply filters to any column. Use the (All) filter to remove any filter criteria and use the Custom filter to filter a column by more than one criterion.

1 Open your project in Task Sheet view and view all subtasks.

2 Select View>Table>Usage from the Menu bar. The relevant columns are displayed.

You can save an AutoFilter as a Custom filter for future use.

3 Click the AutoFilter button on the Toolbar. Down arrows appear on column headings:

ⓘ	Task Name ▼	Work ▼	Duration ▼	Start ▼	Finish ▼
	⊟ **Initiation Stage**	**83 hrs**	**13 days**	**Tue 7/1/03**	**Thu 7/17/03**
	Agree Project Objectiv	8 hrs	1 day	Tue 7/1/03	Tue 7/1/03
◆	Identify Stakeholders	8 hrs	1 day	Wed 7/2/03	Wed 7/2/03
	Identify Project Team	32 hrs	2 days	Thu 7/3/03	Fri 7/4/03
	Identify Business Case	16 hrs	1 day	Mon 7/7/03	Mon 7/7/03
	Analyze the Risks	11 hrs	2.75 days	Thu 7/10/03	Mon 7/14/03
🖽 ✎	Produce Outline Projec	8 hrs	1 day	Thu 7/10/03	Thu 7/10/03
	Project Approval	0 hrs	0 days	Thu 7/17/03	Thu 7/17/03

4 Click the Duration down arrow and select >1 day (greater than 1 day). The view changes to only display tasks greater than 1 day's duration and the column heading is displayed in blue. Change it back to (All).

5 Click the Work down arrow and select Custom. The Custom AutoFilter dialog box opens. In Work, select "is greater than...". Select 12h and click OK. The display is filtered accordingly.

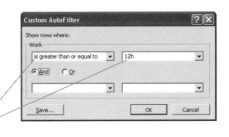

6 Click the AutoFilter button on the Toolbar again to turn it off. All tasks are displayed again.

Filter Criteria

You can specify filter criteria interactively if you often want to make a similar enquiry but with slightly different parameters. This is preferable to creating a large number of custom filters.

For example, you might want to get details of all tasks during the summer to check for any vacation implications:

1 Open your project in Task Sheet view and select View>Table> Schedule from the Menu bar.

2 Select Project>Filtered for>Date Range from the Menu bar. The Date Range dialog box opens:

3 Type "8/1/03" and click OK. The Date Range dialog box opens again for the end date.

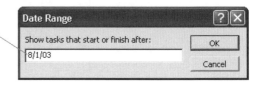

Although the dialog says "...start or finish after", it actually means "...start or finish on or after".

4 Type "8/31/03" and click OK. Now only tasks that are due to be in progress during August are listed:

Task Name	Start	Finish	Late Start	Late Finish
⊟ **Strategy Stage**	**Fri 7/18/03**	**Fri 8/15/03**	**Fri 9/12/03**	**Fri 10/3/03**
Carry out Risk Analysis	Thu 7/31/03	Wed 8/6/03	Wed 9/24/03	Tue 9/30/03
Produce Forward Plan	Wed 8/6/03	Thu 8/7/03	Tue 9/30/03	Wed 10/1/03
⊟ **Report to Management**	**Thu 8/7/03**	**Fri 8/15/03**	**Wed 10/1/03**	**Fri 10/3/03**
Prepare Report	Thu 8/7/03	Fri 8/8/03	Wed 10/1/03	Thu 10/2/03
Present to Management	Fri 8/15/03	Fri 8/15/03	Fri 10/3/03	Fri 10/3/03
⊟ **Analysis Stage**	**Fri 8/15/03**	**Fri 9/5/03**	**Fri 10/3/03**	**Fri 10/24/03**
Agree Requirements	Fri 8/15/03	Fri 8/22/03	Fri 10/3/03	Fri 10/10/03
Select Package	Fri 8/22/03	Fri 8/29/03	Fri 10/10/03	Fri 10/17/03
Purchase Package	Fri 8/29/03	Tue 9/2/03	Fri 10/17/03	Tue 10/21/03

5 Click the Filter down arrow on the Toolbar and select All Tasks. All tasks are again displayed.

Filter by Resource

You can use resource filters to display tasks assigned to a resource. You can also use resource filters to change the resource information for one or more resources.

If the Facilities Group was going to change its name to Premises and you wanted to change all resources, you could use the resource filter to filter by that group name and then change it for all resources in the group.

1 Open your project in Resource Sheet view.

2 Click the Filter down arrow on the Toolbar and select Group... (the three dots indicate further choices).

3 Type in "Facilities" and click OK. Now only the four Facilities resources are displayed.

4 Click the Resource Name column heading to select all resources. Then click the Resource Information button on the Toolbar. The Multiple Resource Information dialog opens.

5 On the General tab, click in the Group field, type "Premises" and click OK. Accept any warnings. All resources will have their Group changed to Premises.

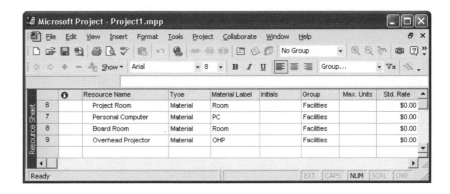

Custom Filters

Custom filters can be created from new or they can be created from an existing filter. The easiest way is to make a copy of an existing filter and then edit it.

The Filter Definition dialog is used to name the filter, select the settings and define the criteria. A filter can have a single criterion or multiple criteria. Where multiple criteria are used they have to be separated by operators such as "And" and "Or" ("And" means both criteria must be met, "Or" means either or both can be met).

I   Open your project in Gantt Chart view and select Project> Filtered For>More Filters. The More Filters dialog box opens (this lists all filters).

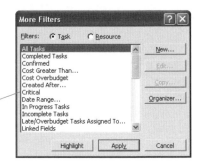

To copy an existing filter, click Copy in the More Filters dialog.

2   Click New. The Filter Definition dialog box opens.

3   Type the name "Start after Sep 1" and select Show in menu.

4   Click in the first row under Field Name, click the down arrow and select Start.

5   Click in the Test column, click the down arrow and select is greater than or equal to.

6   Click in the Value(s) column, type "9/1/03" and click OK. The new filter is shown in the More Filters dialog box.

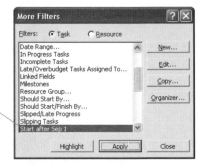

The new filter is also now shown in the drop-down list on the Toolbar.

7   Click Apply and only the tasks from September are displayed.

Sorting

Tasks and resources are usually displayed in ascending ID Number order. However, you can sort by any field or even a combination of fields by specifying sort keys.

1 Open your project in Task Sheet view and show all subtasks.

2 Select View>Table>Usage from the Menu bar.

3 Select Project>Sort>Sort By from the Menu bar. The Sort dialog box opens.

4 Click the Sort by down arrow, select Summary and select Descending. Click the Then by down arrow, select Duration and select Descending. Deselect Keep outline structure and click Sort.

The summary tasks are sorted first in descending sequence followed by the subtasks in descending sequence:

Combining sorting with filters gives you a powerful range of features.

	ⓘ	Task Name	Work	Duration	Start	Finish
32		⊟ **Implementation Stage**	**160 hrs**	**57.75 days**	**Tue 10/28/03**	**Thu 1/22/04**
28		⊟ **Design & Build Stage**	**320 hrs**	**37.25 days**	**Fri 9/5/03**	**Tue 10/28/03**
9		⊟ **Strategy Stage**	**116 hrs**	**20.5 days**	**Fri 7/18/03**	**Fri 8/15/03**
23		⊟ **Analysis Stage**	**80 hrs**	**15 days**	**Fri 8/15/03**	**Fri 9/5/03**
1		⊟ **Initiation Stage**	**83 hrs**	**13 days**	**Tue 7/1/03**	**Thu 7/17/03**
20		⊟ **Report to Management**	**8 hrs**	**6 days**	**Thu 8/7/03**	**Fri 8/15/03**
10		⊟ **Carry out Interviews**	**32 hrs**	**4 days**	**Fri 7/18/03**	**Wed 7/23/03**
31		Change Budget	200 hrs	25 days	Tue 9/23/03	Tue 10/28/03
29		Design	80 hrs	10 days	Fri 9/5/03	Wed 9/17/03
35		Change Budget	80 hrs	10 days	Fri 1/9/04	Thu 1/22/04
24		Agree Requirements	20 hrs	5 days	Fri 8/15/03	Fri 8/22/03
25		Select Package	20 hrs	5 days	Fri 8/22/03	Fri 8/29/03
30		Install Package	40 hrs	5 days	Wed 9/17/03	Tue 9/23/03
33		Train Users	40 hrs	5 days	Tue 10/28/03	Tue 11/4/03
34	▦	Convert to New Package	40 hrs	5 days	Fri 1/2/04	Thu 1/8/04

Highlight Filters

When tasks and resources are filtered, those that do not meet the criteria are hidden from view. Highlight filters can be used so that all tasks or resources remain visible but the tasks or resources that meet the filter criteria are highlighted in blue.

1   Open your project in Gantt Chart view and show all subtasks.

2   Select Project>Filter For>More Filters. The More Filters dialog box opens.

3   Select Resource Group... and click Highlight. Then in the Resource Group dialog box type "Director". The tasks with a resource in the Director group (1.3, 1.4, 2.5 and 2.6) are highlighted in blue:

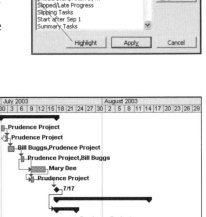

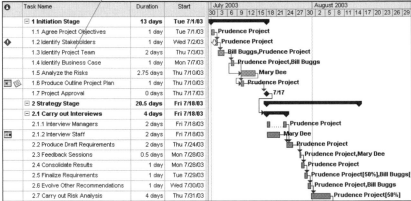

4   Click the Filter down arrow on the Toolbar and select All Tasks. The display returns to normal once again.

Printing Reports

This chapter covers the setup, preview and printing of charts and reports. It deals with headers and footers, scaling reports, previewing and printing.

Finally, it covers the Copy Picture facility which enables you to copy and paste from Project 2002 to another application (typically a word processor for preparing a project report).

Covers

Chapter Thirteen

Printing

If your project is going to be successful, you will need to communicate information on the project and its progress on a regular basis. In addition to the 24 predefined views (which you can print), Project 2002 also contains an additional 22 predefined report formats for printing information about your project.

Project Gantt Chart

The printed project Gantt Chart is probably the most useful tool for communicating basic project progress information to various groups of stakeholders. However, different groups of people will need information presented to them in different ways.

The Project Team

The project team will need detailed information on the current stage, tasks and activities and their progress against schedule. They will also need to see the "big picture" from time to time so that they don't lose sight of the overall project.

Management

Management will usually only require information at the summary level together with details of what problems and issues have occurred, or perhaps might occur.

When faced with choices (such as "Do we increase the scope of the project to include this new area we have uncovered or do we stick with the original schedule?"), you can produce reports that show the answers to the "what if" type of questions.

Types of Report

The types of report that can be produced are as follows:

- Any chart view (using Print from the Toolbar).

- Overviews (summary, top-level and critical tasks).

- Current Activities (tasks due, in progress or slipping).

- Cost, Assignment, Workload or Custom reports.

The Page Setup dialog box allows you to set the page orientation (Portrait or Landscape), adjust margin widths, change scales, create headers and footers and control the flow of information.

Headers and Footers

In addition to the basic information displayed in a report, Project 2002 allows you to create your own headers and footers which are displayed at the top and bottom of every page in a report. These are set up using the Page Setup dialog box.

You can enter any text you like and also include any general system information (page number, date, title, etc.) and a wide range of project level information.

1 Open your project in Gantt Chart view and hide all subtasks.

2 Select File>Page Setup from the Menu bar (to open the Page Setup dialog box) and click the Header tab.

3 Click the Center tab and then click in the text area below it.

4 Click the down arrow next to General, select Company Name and click Add. Then repeat but select Project Title and click Add.

You can click Print Preview to see how it looks (see next topic).

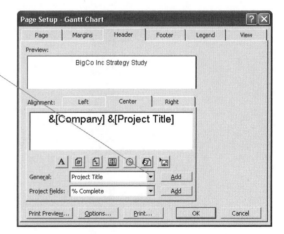

5 Now click the Footer tab and add "Total Page Count" after the page number (put "of" between them). Then click the Left Alignment tab, type "Duration:", select Duration from the Project information drop-down list (below the General list) and click Add. Finally click OK to save the header and footer information.

Previewing Reports

With Project 2002 it is always a good idea to preview a report before printing it. That way you can make sure it will look the way you want, and make any final adjustments to it.

1 Open your project in Gantt Chart view with all subtasks hidden.

2 Click Print Preview on the Toolbar.

3 Print Preview opens and looks something like this:

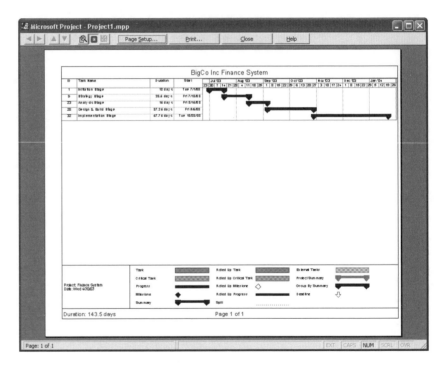

You can always print your current chart view using the Print button.

4 If you move your cursor over the Preview page it changes to a magnifying glass which allows you to zoom in or out.

5 Zoom in and check your header and footer information. (You can use Page Setup to change any details, such as the font size.) Click Close to exit Print Preview.

Print Setup and Scaling

In Project 2002 you can set the paper size and many other details from the Page Setup dialog box. You can also scale reports to get the best fit to a certain number of pages.

1. Open your project in Gantt Chart view, hide all subtasks and select File>Page Setup from the Menu bar. The Page Setup dialog box opens:

2. Select the Page tab then Fit to. Select 1 page wide by 1 page tall.

3. Click in First page number and change its entry to 5.

4. Click Print Preview to see how the print will look so far.

5. In the Print Preview screen click Page Setup to reopen the Page Setup dialog box. Then do the following:

   - Select the Header tab and change the font size to a larger size such as 14 point.

   - Select the Footer tab, change the font size to a larger size such as 12 point and delete the of &[Pages] to get rid of the "of 5" after the page number.

   Click OK to see the revised Print Preview. Continue making adjustments until you are happy with the look and layout of the report.

Printing Reports

There are 22 predefined report formats available in Project 2002, grouped into six categories.

If you don't show all subtasks, they will not appear in your reports.

1 Open your project in Gantt Chart view and show all subtasks. Select View>Reports from the Menu bar. The Reports dialog box opens:

You can also just double-click on Current Activities.

2 Select Current Activities and then click Select. The Current Activity Reports dialog box opens:

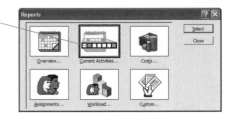

3 Select Unstarted Tasks and then click Edit. The Task Report dialog box opens:

If you don't want to change the standard report, just click Select to preview/print it.

4 Select the Definition tab and then Show summary tasks. Select the Details tab (shown on the facing page).

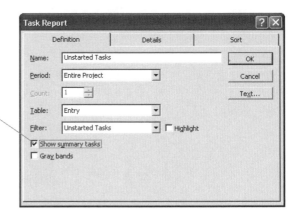

5 Under Assignment, select Notes and Schedule. Under Task, select Notes. Then select Gridlines between details. Click OK.

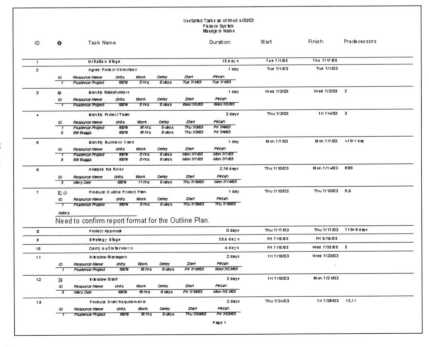

Project 2002 returns you to the Current Activity Reports dialog box (as shown on the facing page).

6 Click Select in the Current Activity Reports dialog box. The report is previewed:

Using these steps and Print Preview, you can explore all the report formats available without needing to print.

7 Click Print and then OK to print the report. Finally click Close to close the Reports dialog box.

Copy Picture

The Copy Picture facility in Project 2002 is one of the
really useful features for producing management reports.
It can be selected from the Copy Picture button
on the Toolbar or through the Edit menu.

1 Open your project in Gantt Chart view and select Show>Outline
Level 1 from the Toolbar.

2 Adjust the panes to give approximately the required picture.
Then click the Copy Picture button.

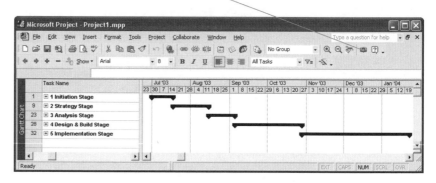

If the picture is large or will not fit easily into another application, Project 2002 will alert you.

3 Select For
printer in the
Render image
section. Under
Timescale,
enter your
project's start
and end dates
in the From:
and To: boxes.
Click OK.

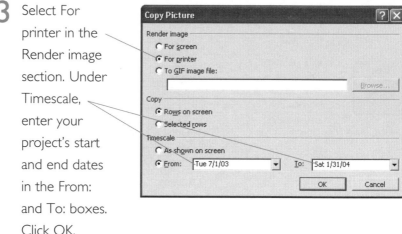

4 Open your target application (Word, etc.) and paste the picture
into your report using the standard Paste command.

Tracking Progress

This chapter introduces progress tracking and entering progress information. It explains the different types of progress information and how to deal with them.

Covers

Chapter Fourteen

Progress Tracking

Up to now, you have been planning your project, allocating resources to it and then scheduling when things will happen. Once the project is actually under way, though, you need to start tracking progress against your plan and schedule.

You enter information about progress by using actual start and completion dates as well as effort expended by resource.

If tasks are completed ahead of schedule, you can then decide if you want to bring other tasks forward. If tasks are running late, you can decide what actions you can take to help.

Again, the Gantt Chart is the most effective way of tracking progress as it can show actual against the plan.

Before you begin to enter actual information, complete your plan in as much detail as you are able, using change budgets to allow for the unknown. Once you are happy with the plan you can set a baseline and then start progress tracking.

Project 2002 stores information under three headings:

Baseline	the plan dates which are compared with the actual and scheduled dates.
Actual	completed tasks or part-completed tasks.
Schedule	tasks that have not yet been started or work remaining on part-completed tasks.

The frequency with which you enter your information is up to you, but typically you would get progress details from the people working on the project at the end of each week.

As you enter your actual data the project is recalculated and rescheduled. So start at the earliest tasks on the schedule and work through. Once you have input all the actual information and seen the impact on the schedule you can re-evaluate the project and make any adjustments required to the project tasks to deal with issues that have arisen.

Progress Information

In addition to actual start and finish dates you can also input progress information on the percentage completed, actual and remaining duration, actual and remaining work and actual and remaining cost.

Depending on the type of information you input, Project 2002 will calculate the other relevant information.

If you input a task completion date, Project 2002 will set the actual start date to the scheduled start date and the actual duration to the difference between the start date and actual completion date.

The most accurate way of recording progress is to input the actual work done. This should be recorded by all the people resources you have working on the project. If this is less than the estimate for the task, Project 2002 will then calculate the work remaining as the difference between the actual work done and the original estimate.

While Project 2002's calculation of the work to completion may be acceptable at the beginning of a task, it is far more accurate to get people to record their own estimates of the work required to complete their tasks at the same time as they record the work done. You can then input this information and get a picture of the way the project is really going.

You can also input actual duration and, if that is less than the scheduled duration, Project 2002 calculates the remaining duration as the difference. If the task is actually completed in less than the scheduled duration, you need to set the remaining duration to zero. If it is going to be completed in less or more time you can again input your expected duration.

In the same way, you can enter actual and remaining costs.

You can input this task progress information in a number of views including Gantt Chart, Task Usage and Resource Usage views.

Completed Work

One a task has been completed, the easiest way to enter that information is simply by telling Project 2002 that the task is completed.

1   Open your project in Gantt Chart view and select Task 1.1 (Agree Project Objectives).

2   Select Tools>Tracking>Update Tasks from the Menu bar. The Update Tasks dialog box appears:

3   Click the Finish down arrow, select the scheduled finish date (7/1/03) and click OK.

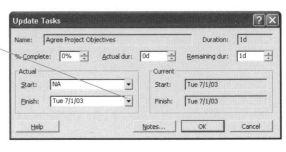

After step 3, the task is completed and the Information field is checked. The task is also removed from the Critical Path (it reverts to blue) and a progress bar (a black line) is displayed through it.

4   Select Tools>Tracking>Update Tasks from the Menu bar again. The actual start and finish dates are entered, the task is shown as 100% complete, the actual duration is shown as 1 day and the remaining duration is set to zero.

5   Click Cancel. Position the cursor over the task's Information field.

The date completed information pops up.

Part Completed Work

Where a number of hours or days of work have been carried out on a task but the task is not yet fully completed, you can enter the actual work carried out:

1 Open your project in Task Usage view and select Task 3 (Identify Stakeholders).

2 Select Format>Details>Actual Work from the Menu bar. Actual Work fields are displayed underneath the estimated Work fields.

Click the Go To Selected Task button, if necessary, to bring the selected task into view.

	Task Name	Work	Details	T	W	T
1	⊟ **Initiation Stage**	**83 hrs**	Work	8h	8h	16h
			Act. W	8h		
2	⊟ Agree Project Objectives	8 hrs	Work	8h		
			Act. W	8h		
	Prudence Project	*8 hrs*	Work	8h		
			Act. W	8h		
3	⊟ Identify Stakeholders	8 hrs	Work		8h	
			Act. W			
	Prudence Project	*8 hrs*	Work		8h	
			Act. W		5	

3 Click in the Actual Work field for the task, type "5" and press enter. Accept any constraint warnings received and continue.

	Task Name	Work	Details	T	W	T
1	⊟ **Initiation Stage**	**83 hrs**	Work	8h	5h	13h
			Act. W	8h	5h	
2	⊟ Agree Project Objectives	8 hrs	Work	8h		
			Act. W	8h		
	Prudence Project	*8 hrs*	Work	8h		
			Act. W	8h		
3	⊟ Identify Stakeholders	8 hrs	Work		5h	3h
			Act. W		5h	
	Prudence Project	*8 hrs*	Work		5h	3h
			Act. W		5h	

The actual hours are entered, the work is rescheduled from 8 to 5 hours and the remaining 3 hours are rescheduled the next day.

Percentage Completed

There is a certain amount of risk involved in using percentage completed as the measure of work done on a task. It is human nature for most people to be optimistic about their progress so a measure of actual work done and estimate of work to completion is usually more accurate. However, it will sometimes be appropriate to use percentage completed where it's not practical to track work more closely.

1 Open your project in Task Sheet view (by selecting View>More Views>Task Sheet from the Menu bar and clicking Apply).

2 Select View>Table>Tracking from the Menu bar.

3 Select View>Toolbars>Tracking from the Menu bar.

4 Select Task 4 (Identify Project Team) and click the 75% Complete button on the Tracking Toolbar.

`75`

If your tasks are still sorted from a previous topic, select Project> Sort>Sort By> Reset>Sort from the Menu bar.

The Actual Start date is entered as scheduled. The percentage completed is set to 75% and the Actual Duration, Remaining Duration, Actual Cost and Actual Work fields are all updated:

	Task Name	Act. Start	Act. Finish	% Comp.	Phys. % Comp.	Act. Dur.	Rem. Dur.	Act. Cost	Act. Work
1	⊟ Initiation Stage	Tue 7/1/03	NA	38%	0%	4.99 days	8.01 days	$980.00	37 hrs
2	Agree Project Objectives	Tue 7/1/03	Tue 7/1/03	100%	0%	1 day	0 days	$160.00	8 hrs
3	Identify Stakeholders	Wed 7/2/03	NA	73%	0%	1 day	0.38 days	$100.00	5 hrs
4	Identify Project Team	Thu 7/3/03	NA	75%	0%	1.5 days	0.5 days	$720.00	24 hrs
5	Identify Business Case	NA	NA	0%	0%	0 days	1 day	$0.00	0 hrs

You can input and adjust any percentage figure using the Update Tasks dialog.

5 Select View>Gantt Chart from the Menu bar. The part-completed tasks are shown with progress bars:

	ⓘ	Task Name	Duration	Start	Jun 30, '03 S M T W T F S
1		⊟ 1 Initiation Stage	13 days	Tue 7/1/03	
2	✓	1.1 Agree Project Objectives	1 day	Tue 7/1/03	Prudence
3	◆	1.2 Identify Stakeholders	1.38 days	Wed 7/2/03	Prude
4		1.3 Identify Project Team	2 days	Thu 7/3/03	
5		1.4 Identify Business Case	1 day	Mon 7/7/03	
6		1.5 Analyze the Risks	2.75 days	Thu 7/10/03	

Duration Completed

In the same way as you can enter actual work done, you can also enter actual and remaining duration for a task.

1 Open your project in Gantt Chart view and select Task 1.5 (Analyze the Risks).

2 Select Tools>Tracking>Update Tasks from the Menu bar. The Update Tasks dialog box opens:

If you have the Tracking Toolbar displayed you can click the Update Tasks button.

3 Click the Actual dur: up arrow to display 1 day then click OK. If you get a task scheduling conflict warning select

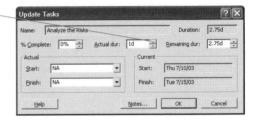

Continue. The task is updated on the Gantt Chart.

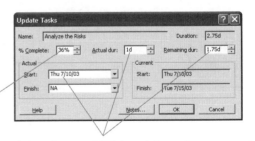

	❶	Task Name	Duration	Start	Jun 30, '03 S M T W T F S	Jul 7, '03 S M T W T F S
1		⊟ **1 Initiation Stage**	**13 days**	**Tue 7/1/03**		
2	✓	1.1 Agree Project Objectives	1 day	Tue 7/1/03	Prudence Project	
3	◆	1.2 Identify Stakeholders	1.38 days	Wed 7/2/03	Prudence Project	
4		1.3 Identify Project Team	2 days	Thu 7/3/03		Bill Buggs,Prud
5		1.4 Identify Business Case	1 day	Mon 7/7/03		Prudence P
6		1.5 Analyze the Risks	2.75 days	Thu 7/10/03		
7	▣ 🗒	1.6 Produce Outline Project Plan	1 day	Thu 7/10/03		Prud
8		1.7 Project Approval	0 days	Thu 7/17/03		

4 Select Tools> Tracking>Update Tasks again from the Menu bar. Note that the % Complete is set to 36%, Actual dur: to 1 day, Remaining dur: to 1.75d and Actual: Start is set to the scheduled start date. Click Cancel and save your project file.

Entering Costs

Normally Project 2002 calculates actual costs for you based on the actual work and the cost details you have entered for the resource. However, you can also enter actual cost details directly:

1 Select Tools>Options from the Menu bar. The Options dialog box opens:

2 Click the Calculation tab.

3 Clear Actual costs are always calculated by Microsoft Project and click OK.

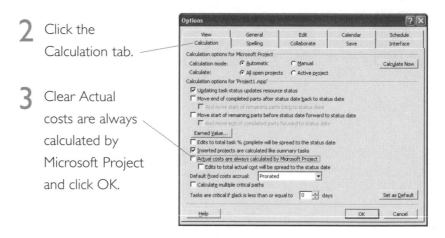

4 Select View>Task Usage from the Menu bar.

5 Select View>Table>Tracking from the Menu bar.

6 Select Format>Details>Actual Cost from the Menu bar.

Note that you can only enter actual costs for completed tasks.

7 In Task 2, click in the Actual Cost field. Type "200" and press Enter.

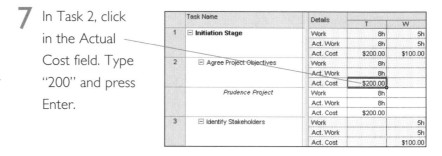

8 Close your file without saving it.

Updating as Scheduled

One or more tasks that have been started and/or completed as scheduled can be updated using the Update As Scheduled button on the Tracking Toolbar or the Update Project dialog box.

1   Open your project in Gantt Chart view.

2   Select Tools>Tracking>Update Project to open the Update Project dialog box:

3   Select Update work as complete through, set the date to 7/10/03 and click OK. If you get a scheduling conflict

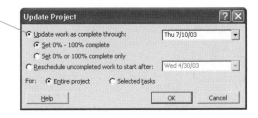

warning select Continue and click OK. The tasks are now all shown as completed up to July 10 and Task 1.5 (Analyze the Risks) is shown as part completed up to July 10:

❶	Task Name	Duration	Start	Jun 30, '03 S M T W T F S	Jul 7, '03 S M T W T F S S
	⊟ **1 Initiation Stage**	**13 days**	**Tue 7/1/03**		
✓	1.1 Agree Project Objectives	1 day	Tue 7/1/03	▬▬Prudence Project	
✓	1.2 Identify Stakeholders	1.38 days	Wed 7/2/03	▬▬Prudence Project	
✓	1.3 Identify Project Team	2 days	Thu 7/3/03	▬▬▬Bill Buggs,Pruden	
✓	1.4 Identify Business Case	1 day	Mon 7/7/03	▬▬Prudence Proj	
	1.5 Analyze the Risks	2.75 days	Thu 7/10/03		
✓ 📝	1.6 Produce Outline Project Plan	1 day	Thu 7/10/03	▬▬Pruden	

4   Select Task 1.5 (Analyze the Risks) and click the Update Tasks button on the Tracking Toolbar.

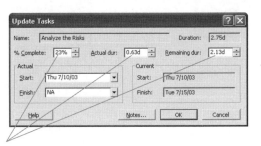

The task is shown at 23% completed with 0.63 days actual and 2.13 days remaining. Click Cancel.

Actual v. Baseline

Having set the project baseline, you can monitor your actual progress against the baseline at any time. The baseline and actual figures can be displayed in a number of tables, through the use of filters and in the Tracking Gantt Chart view.

1 In Gantt Chart view select Task 1.5 (Analyze the Risks) and click the Update Tasks button on the Tracking Toolbar. The Update Tasks dialog box opens:

You can use the up and down arrows to step through one day at a time.

2 Increase the Actual dur: setting to 1 day and the Remaining dur: setting to 4 days. Click OK.

You may receive a scheduling conflict warning. If so, select Continue and the project will be rescheduled.

Update Tasks			? X
Name:	Analyze the Risks	Duration:	2.75d
% Complete: 23%	Actual dur: 1d	Remaining dur: 4d	
Actual		**Current**	
Start: Thu 7/10/03		Start: Thu 7/10/03	
Finish: NA		Finish: Tue 7/15/03	
Help		Notes... OK Cancel	

3 Select View>Table>Work from the Menu bar and the Work Table view opens. Note that:

Work = Actual + Remaining

Variance = Work − Baseline

Use the Filter down arrow on the Toolbar to display over-budget or slipping tasks.

	Task Name	Work	Baseline	Variance	Actual	Remaining
1	⊟ **1 Initiation Stage**	**87.5 hrs**	**83 hrs**	**4.5 hrs**	**73.8 hrs**	**13.7 hrs**
2	1.1 Agree Project Objectives	8 hrs	8 hrs	0 hrs	8 hrs	0 hrs
3	1.2 Identify Stakeholders	8 hrs	8 hrs	0 hrs	8 hrs	0 hrs
4	1.3 Identify Project Team	32 hrs	32 hrs	0 hrs	32 hrs	0 hrs
5	1.4 Identify Business Case	16 hrs	16 hrs	0 hrs	16 hrs	0 hrs
6	1.5 Analyze the Risks	15.5 hrs	11 hrs	4.5 hrs	1.8 hrs	13.7 hrs
7	1.6 Produce Outline Project Plan	8 hrs	8 hrs	0 hrs	8 hrs	0 hrs
8	1.7 Project Approval	0 hrs	0 hrs	0 hrs	0 hrs	0 hrs

4 Select View>Table>Cost to see the Actual and Baseline cost, and View>Table>Variance to see the start and finish date variance from the Baseline.

Tracking Gantt Chart

The Tracking Gantt Chart gives a graphical representation of the actual state of the project compared to the baseline.

1 Select View>Tracking Gantt from the Menu bar and adjust your view so that it looks like the following:

	ⓘ	Task Name	Duration	Start	Jun 30, '03	Jul 7, '03	Jul 14, '03
					S M T W T F S	S M T W T F S	S M T W T F S S
1		⊟ Initiation Stage	13 days	Tue 7/1/03			65%
2	✓	Agree Project Objectives	1 day	Tue 7/1/03	100%		
3	✓	Identify Stakeholders	1.38 days	Wed 7/2/03	100%		
4	✓	Identify Project Team	2 days	Thu 7/3/03		100%	
5	✓	Identify Business Case	1 day	Mon 7/7/03		100%	
6		Analyze the Risks	5 days	Thu 7/10/03			20%
7	✓🗎	Produce Outline Project Plan	1 day	Thu 7/10/03		100%	
8		Project Approval	0 days	Thu 7/17/03			7/17

Note the following:

- Actual progress is shown as a hatched line underneath summary Task 1 (Initiation).

- The baseline is shown in gray beneath the actual and scheduled task bars.

- For Task 2 (Agree Project Objectives) the actual and baseline are the same since the task was completed to schedule.

- Task 3 (Identify Stakeholders) started on schedule but was completed 0.38 days late.

- Tasks 4 and 5 were completed to their estimated duration but were started late (due to Task 3) and thus finished late.

- Task 6 started late and will be finished later still, while Task 7 was completed on time.

- Finally, there is no baseline milestone (an empty diamond) as the scheduled milestone (a solid diamond) is also the baseline (i.e. it is still on schedule).

Having some lag time in your schedule allows you to cope with task delays without throwing out the schedule.

2 Double-click on the link between Tasks 6 and 7 and change the dependency from a finish-to-start to a start-to-start to remove the inconsistency.

Project Statistics

The Project Statistics dialog box gives you summary level information for the whole project.

1 Select Project>Project Information from the Menu bar. The Project Information dialog box opens:

2 Click Statistics. The Project Statistics dialog box opens:

You can also click the Project Statistics button on the Tracking Toolbar.

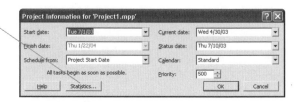

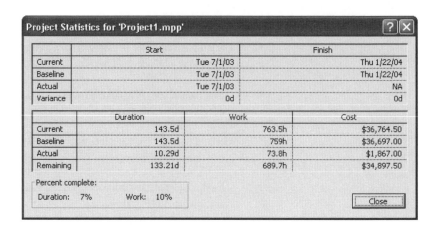

	Start	Finish
Current	Tue 7/1/03	Thu 1/22/04
Baseline	Tue 7/1/03	Thu 1/22/04
Actual	Tue 7/1/03	NA
Variance	0d	0d

	Duration	Work	Cost
Current	143.5d	763.5h	$36,764.50
Baseline	143.5d	759h	$36,697.00
Actual	10.29d	73.8h	$1,867.00
Remaining	133.21d	689.7h	$34,897.50

Percent complete:
Duration: 7%   Work: 10%

The top section   shows the current, baseline, actual and variance for the start and finish dates.

The middle section   shows statistics on the project's duration, work and cost. Note that, in spite of some of the tasks in Stage 1 (Initiation) running late, we have kept the project on schedule as a result of the lag time. However, we are currently over-budget on the Work and Cost.

The final section   shows the overall percentage completed in Duration and Work.

Progress Lines

Progress Lines can be drawn on the Gantt or Tracking Gantt Chart at any date to show the actual or expected progress at that date.

They work by linking the tasks that are scheduled to be started, completed or in progress on that date. Tasks that are behind schedule result in peaks to the left of the line, and tasks that are ahead of schedule result in peaks to the right of the line.

1 Open your project in Gantt Chart view and make sure the Tracking Toolbar is displayed.

2 Click the Add Progress Line button on the Tracking Toolbar.
The cursor changes to a jagged line with an arrow on either side.

3 Move the cursor over the Gantt Chart until the pop-up box displays a Progress Date of July 14.

Progress Line	
Progress Date:	Mon 7/14/03
Click the mouse to display a progress line on this date	

4 Click on that date and the progress line will be displayed on the chart:

ⓘ	Task Name	Duration	Start
	⊟ **1 Initiation Stage**	**13 days**	**Tue 7/1/03**
✓	1.1 Agree Project Objectives	1 day	Tue 7/1/03
✓	1.2 Identify Stakeholders	1.38 days	Wed 7/2/03
✓	1.3 Identify Project Team	2 days	Thu 7/3/03
✓	1.4 Identify Business Case	1 day	Mon 7/7/03
	1.5 Analyze the Risks	5 days	Thu 7/10/03
✓ 📝	1.6 Produce Outline Project Plan	1 day	Thu 7/10/03
	1.7 Project Approval	0 days	Thu 7/17/03

You can place multiple progress lines on a chart and delete any of them in the Progress Lines dialog box.

5 To remove a progress line, double-click the line and the Progress Lines dialog box opens. Click Delete then click OK and the progress line is removed.

When is a Task Completed?

This chapter has concentrated on tracking your project's progress by entering details of tasks and work completed. But one of the difficult decisions facing a project manager is, exactly when do you treat a task as completed?

The old quotation used to be "The job's not over until the paperwork's done". This was usually accompanied by a picture of a small child on a potty!

The more formal answer is that the task has been completed when everything that needs to be done has been done. If the task was to produce something tangible like a report or specification, then the task is not completed until the product has been produced and formally signed off. This should include any quality control or management approval.

The "80% Completed" Syndrome

Experienced project managers will be well aware of the "80% Completed" syndrome. This is a reflection of people's basic optimism when estimating the work remaining to complete a task. This is the reason why using percentage completed figures is not usually very accurate.

Be Realistic

So, to be realistic, use the actual work effort used and the estimated work to completion. In the early stages of a task these should add up to the work estimated for the task. As the task progresses they should begin to show if the task is going to take more or less work than the original estimate. And there should be no sudden, last-minute surprises.

If someone is estimating that they will be completing a task to plan until the very last moment and then it suddenly increases, they were not being realistic. As the project manager, you should feed that back to them (in a constructive way) so that they will, hopefully, be more accurate in future tasks.

Finally, if they have used up all the estimated time and the task is still not formally completed or signed off, then they should still be showing some work as their estimate to completion.

Customizing

This chapter introduces the customizing of tables, views, reports and fields in Project 2002. It also shows you how to share customized items between projects.

Covers

Chapter Fifteen

Customizing Project 2002

Project 2002 has a large number of predefined tables, views, reports and fields. These will probably cover most requirements for most projects. However, if you do need a different table, view, report or field, Project 2002 allows you to customize or create new ones. In addition to being able to change the sequence of columns in a table, view or report, there are over 200 different fields holding information that you can access and custom fields that you can use for any other information.

Tables

Tables are made up of columns and rows of information and there are 17 predefined task tables and 10 predefined resource tables available in Project 2002. If none of these match your requirements you can create your own custom tables to include exactly the information you require. You can also combine your custom tables with predefined or custom filters.

Views

Project 2002 contains 24 predefined views which display schedule information and allow you to edit it. Some of these views are single views and some are combination views. Single views consist of a screen, table and filter. Combination views combine 2 single views on the same screen by splitting them one above the other. Custom views can be based on any combination.

Reports

Project 2002 contains 22 predefined reports split into 5 report groups. Custom reports can be based on any of these existing reports or they can be created completely from new. When you create a new report, it can be based on one of 4 report templates: Task Report, Resource Report, Monthly Calendar Report and Crosstab Report.

Fields

Project 2002 contains the facility for 130 custom fields which you can use to hold additional information, carry out calculations or hold graphical indicators. These fields cover cost, date, duration, finish, flag, number, start and text data and outline codes.

Custom Tables

Custom tables can be created from new but it is usually easier to copy an existing table and then edit it.

1 Open your project in Gantt Chart view, select View>Table> More Tables>Summary from the Menu bar, then click Copy. The Table Definition dialog box opens with a copy of the Summary table displayed.

2 Type "Project Summary Table" as the name.

3 In the Field Name column, select Duration and click Delete Row. The row is deleted from the definitions. Now delete Finish and Cost in the same way.

4 Now select %Complete and click Insert Row. Click the down arrow, select Actual Start and press Tab. The default values are inserted for the other fields. Now insert Actual Work in front of %Complete.

You can also press Enter or select another field to insert the default values.

5 Select Work and click Cut Row. Select Actual Work and click Paste Row.

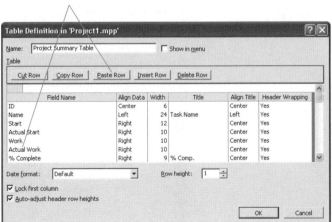

6 Click OK and then click Apply. The new table is applied to your Gantt Chart view.

Custom Views

Custom views can be created as single views or as combination views. First we will create a new single view:

1. Open your project, select View>More Views and click New. The Define New View dialog opens:

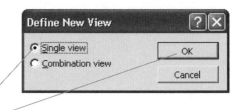

2. Make sure Single view is selected and click OK. The View Definition dialog box opens:

3. Type the name "Project Progress". In subsequent fields, change the settings to: Task Sheet; Project Summary Table; No Group; and Incomplete Tasks. Click OK. The More Views dialog displays again.

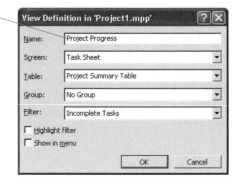

4. Ensure Project Progress is selected and click Apply. The new Project Progress single view is displayed with all incomplete tasks (tasks that are in progress or not yet started) displayed:

		Task Name	Start	Actual Start	Work	Actual Work	% Comp.
	1	⊟ **Initiation Stage**	**Tue 7/1/03**	**Tue 7/1/03**	**87.5 hrs**	**73.8 hrs**	**65%**
	6	Analyze the Risks	Thu 7/10/03	Thu 7/10/03	15.5 hrs	1.8 hrs	20%
	8	Project Approval	Thu 7/17/03	NA	0 hrs	0 hrs	0%
	9	⊟ **Strategy Stage**	**Fri 7/18/03**	**NA**	**116 hrs**	**0 hrs**	**0%**
	10	⊟ **Carry out Interviews**	**Fri 7/18/03**	**NA**	**32 hrs**	**0 hrs**	**0%**
	11	Interview Managers	Fri 7/18/03	NA	16 hrs	0 hrs	0%
	12	Interview Staff	Fri 7/18/03	NA	16 hrs	0 hrs	0%
	13	Produce Draft Requirements	Thu 7/24/03	NA	16 hrs	0 hrs	0%
	14	Feedback Sessions	Mon 7/28/03	NA	8 hrs	0 hrs	0%
	15	Consolidate Results	Mon 7/28/03	NA	8 hrs	0 hrs	0%
	16	Finalize Requirements	Tue 7/29/03	NA	8 hrs	0 hrs	0%
	17	Evolve Other Recommendations	Wed 7/30/03	NA	16 hrs	0 hrs	0%
	18	Carry out Risk Analysis	Thu 7/31/03	NA	16 hrs	0 hrs	0%

Combination Views

To create a combination view we can use our new custom view and combine it with another view:

1 Select View>More Views from the Menu bar and click New.

2 Select Combination view and click OK.

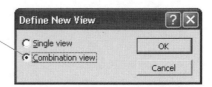

3 Type the name "Progress Review". In Top, select Detail Gantt. In Bottom, select Project Progress. Click OK and then Apply in More Views. The new combination view is displayed:

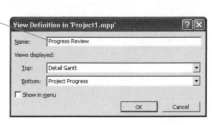

Select Show in menu if you want the new view to show when you click View on the Menu bar.

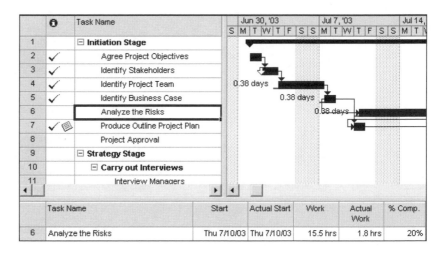

4 Move up and down the tasks in the top pane and the relevant task progress details are displayed in the bottom pane.

5 To display details of several tasks in the bottom pane, select multiple tasks by dragging across them in the top pane.

Custom Reports

While you can always produce a custom report by starting with an existing report which is close to your requirements and then customizing it, you may sometimes want to produce a completely new report.

1 Select View>Reports>Custom and click Select. The Custom Reports dialog box opens:

2 Select Project Summary (notice that the Copy button is not selectable) and click New.

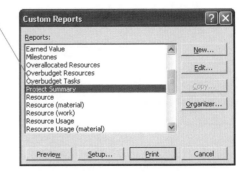

3 Select Crosstab and click OK. The Crosstab Report dialog opens:

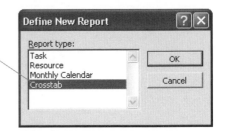

4 Select the Definition tab. Type the name "Weekly Project Costs". Under Row, select Tasks and Cost.

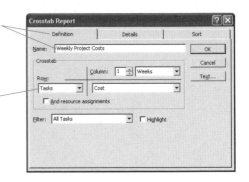

5 Select the Details tab (shown at the top of the facing page).

6 On the Details tab, select Column totals and click OK. The Custom Reports dialog is displayed:

7 Select Weekly Project Costs and click Preview.

8 Your report should look something like the following:

Weekly Project Costs as of Wed 4/30/03
Finance System

	6/30	7/7	7/14	7/21	7/28	8/4
Agree Project Objectives	$160.00					
Identify Stakeholders	$160.00					
Identify Project Team	$780.00	$180.00				
Identify Business Case		$400.00				
Analyze the Risks		$72.00	$160.50			
Produce Outline Project Plan		$160.00				
Project Approval						
Interview Managers			$160.00	$160.00		
Interview Staff			$120.00	$120.00		
Produce Draft Requirements				$320.00		
Feedback Sessions					$140.00	
Consolidate Results					$160.00	
Finalize Requirements					$240.00	
Evolve Other Recommendations					$480.00	
Carry out Risk Analysis					$120.00	$200.00
Produce Forward Plan						$80.00
Prepare Report						$120.00
Present to Management						
Agree Requirements						
Select Package						
Purchase Package						
Change Budget						
Design						
Install Package						
Change Budget						
Train Users						
Convert to New Package						
Change Budget						
Total	$1,100.00	$812.00	$440.50	$600.00	$1,140.00	$400.00

Custom Fields

Project 2002 allows you to define, store and manipulate custom data, set up lists of acceptable values (value lists) to make data entry more accurate, set formulae to perform calculations on the data and set graphic indicators to represent data. When you create a custom field you are actually using and defining an existing field that contains one type of project information.

1 To work with custom fields, select Tools>Customize>Fields from the Menu bar. The Customize Fields dialog box opens:

2 To associate a risk level with each task we will use a custom field, so select Task and Text (note the other field types available).

3 Select Text 1 from the list and click Rename. The Rename Field dialog box opens:

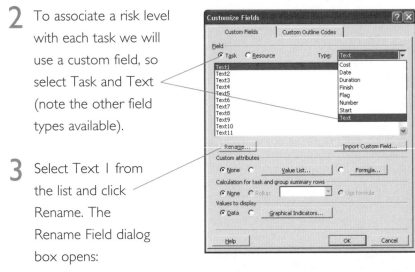

You can also set formulae in a custom field. These can operate on any Project 2002 fields and utilize native Visual Basic functions. The formula syntax is the same as for Microsoft Access.

4 Type "Risk Level" and click OK.

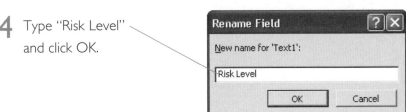

Custom Fields: Value Lists

5 Now click the Value List button as we need to predefine a list of acceptable values for the field. The Value List dialog box opens (shown at top of the facing page).

6 Type in the values shown (High, Medium, Low and No Risk).

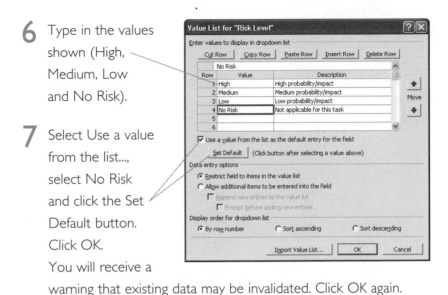

7 Select Use a value from the list..., select No Risk and click the Set Default button. Click OK. You will receive a warning that existing data may be invalidated. Click OK again.

8 To use our new custom field we need to create a new table. In Gantt Chart view select View>Table>More Tables>Copy from the Toolbar. The Table Definition dialog box opens. Type "Risk Management" in the Name field. Select field name Duration and rename it to "Text 1 (Risk Level)". Use these settings: Align Data – Left; Width – 7; and Title – Risk. Click OK and Apply. The new Risk column is displayed.

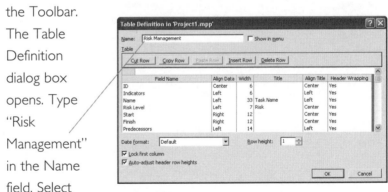

9 Select some of the incomplete tasks and apply risk levels to them (Low, Medium, High or No Risk).

Graphic Indicators

You need to have completed the previous topic before starting this one.

Graphic indicators ("traffic signals" as they are sometimes called) are small colored images that can be assigned to display in custom fields based on the value in the field, a value list selection or a formula calculation result.

1 Open your project in Gantt Chart view and select View>Tables>More Tables>Risk Management. Click Apply to get the risks into view. It should be like the following:

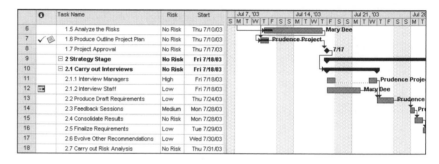

We changed Text 1 to Risk Level.

2 Select Tools>Customize>Fields>Risk Level from the Toolbar and click the Graphic Indicators button.

3 In the Graphic Indicators dialog, select these settings: Test – equals; Value – High; and Image – the red circle. Then do the same for the other values using yellow, green and white circles. Click OK and OK again.

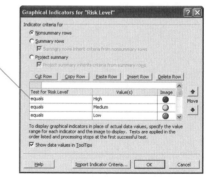

You can change things like reducing the width of the column and centering it by double-clicking the column header.

4 Your risks should now be shown as traffic lights similar to the illustration here.

Sharing Custom Items

Any custom tables, views, reports, fields, value lists or formulae that you create in Project 2002 are stored in the host project file. However, you can make these items available to other projects by using the Organizer.

1 Open your project file and click the New button on the Toolbar. A new blank project is created. If the Project Information dialog box opens click Cancel.

2 Select File>Save As from the Menu bar and save the file as "Share Test".

3 Select View>Table>More Tables from the Menu bar and click Organizer. The Organizer dialog box opens at the Tables tab.

4 In the Tables available in field, select your project.

5 Select Risk Management and click Copy. The Risk Management Table is copied to the new file.

6 Click Close and the More Tables dialog box is displayed. Ensure Tables: Task is selected.

7 Select Risk Management and click Apply. The Risk Management Table is applied to the view:

ⓘ	Task Name	Risk	Start	Jun 2, '03						
				S	M	T	W	T	F	S

A Word of Caution

Although Project 2002 lets you customize and change just about every table, view and report, it is good practice to use a copy of a predefined item and not change the predefined items.

That way, if you make a mistake you can just delete the new item and start again.

Murphy has a word of caution as well:

Murphy's 2nd Law

Anything you try to change will take much longer and cost much more than you thought

Murphy's Second Law applies to just about everything and projects in particular. If your project involves computers, it is widely believed that the impact of Murphy's Second Law doubles.

On the subject of Murphy, here's another relevant one:

Murphy's 3rd Law

If everything seems to be going well, you obviously don't know what's going on

Linking and Exporting

This chapter explains hyperlinks and how to create them. It goes on to cover the creation of HTML and GIF files for publishing on the Web, and also shows you how to export to XML and other file formats. It finishes with an example which uses Excel to display project data.

Covers

Chapter Sixteen

Using Hyperlinks

Hyperlinks (hypertext links) were developed on the World Wide Web and provide a simple way to jump from inside one document to another. With a hyperlink, you can jump to another document on your own computer, your Local Area Network or anywhere on the Web (if you have an Internet connection).

With a hyperlink, you can even open the document you are linking to at any particular point that has a reference.

To follow a hyperlink you just click on it. Pausing your cursor over a hyperlink will usually display some information about it, such as its address in the form of a Uniform Resource Locator (URL):

When inserting a hyperlink, always check that the destination document exists!

http://www.carroll.co.uk/updates.htm

or a local or network file location:

C:\My Documents\project notes.doc

In Project 2002, you can create a hyperlink to another document on any task/resource/assignment via the Insert Hyperlink button.

The hyperlink symbol is displayed in the Indicators field and the hyperlink details are stored in the Hyperlink field. You can also insert a hyperlink in a text column on a sheet view.

HTML

Documents published on the World Wide Web are written in a language called HyperText Markup Language (HTML) which is read and interpreted by a program called a Web browser. Microsoft Internet Explorer is one of the most widely used Web browsers. If you have Microsoft Internet Explorer or another Web browser on your computer, clicking on a hypertext link to a HTML document in Project 2002 will open your browser and then open the HTML document in it. Closing it will return you to Project 2002.

Word or Excel documents

If the hypertext link is to a Word or Excel document on your computer or network, Project 2002 will open Word or Excel and then open the selected document in that program. Closing it will return you to Project 2002.

Inserting a Hyperlink

Adding a hypertext link to a project is very straightforward:

1 Create the following simple HTML file using a text editor:

You can use Windows Notepad as your text editor.

```
<html>
<head>
<title>Simple HTML File</title>
</head>
<body>
A simple HTML file.
</body>
</html>
```

Save the file as "simple.htm" (note the .htm extension).

2 Open your project in Gantt Chart view, select Task 6 (Analyze the Risks) and click the Insert Hyperlink button on the Toolbar. The Insert Hyperlink dialog box opens:

3 Click the Browse button, locate your HTML file and click OK. The hypertext symbol is inserted in the Indicator field.

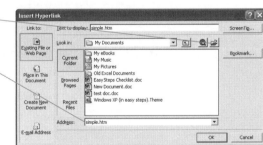

If you don't have a Web browser, create a link to a Word or Excel file. Failing this, link to some other type of file.

4 Pause your cursor over the hypertext symbol. The cursor changes to a pointing finger and the file name pops up.

5 Click on the link to jump to the file. Your browser opens and displays the file. Click Back (or close the browser) to return.

Publishing to HTML

Project data can be saved in HTML format for publishing as Web pages on the Internet or on an internal Intranet. While you can't save the entire project as a HTML file, you can save data from it.

Data is saved using import/export maps which determine which fields of data will be exported.

1 Open your project and select File>Save As Web Page from the Menu bar. Click on Save in the Save As dialog. The Export Wizard opens.

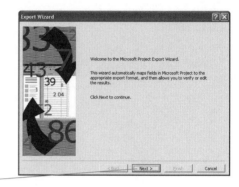

2 Click Next.

3 The Wizard asks you if you want to create a new map or use an existing one. Select New map and click Next. The Map Options dialog box opens.

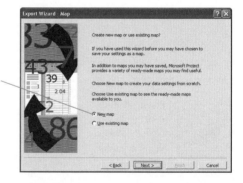

4 Select Tasks then Export header row/Import includes headers. Click Next. The Task Mapping dialog box opens (see the facing page).

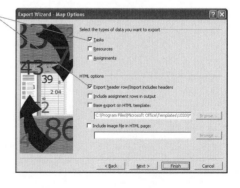

Note you can include an image (GIF) file in this step. See page 202 for how to create a GIF file.

5 Select Summary Tasks as the export filter. Select ID, Name, Duration, Start and % Complete and click Next. The End of Map Definition dialog box opens.

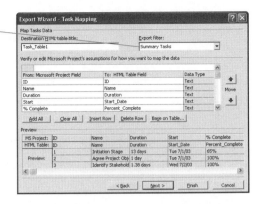

6 If you want to save this map for reuse, click Save Map. Give it a name then click Finish. The HTML file is saved into the selected directory.

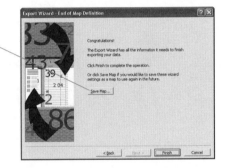

7 View the file in your Web browser:

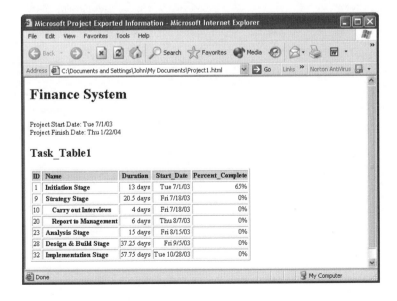

Copying to GIF Files

Although export maps are useful and can be edited, you can only export data to HTML files. If you want to export a picture like a Gantt Chart, you need to export it as a GIF (Graphic Image Format) file.

This is done through the Copy Picture facility:

1 Open your project in Gantt Chart view.

2 Click the Copy Picture button on the Toolbar. The Copy Picture dialog box opens:

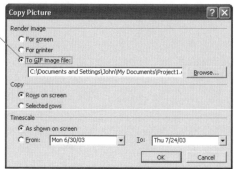

3 Select To GIF image file, Rows on screen and As shown on screen. Click OK.

4 Now view the GIF file using your Task browser or other suitable utility. It should look like the following:

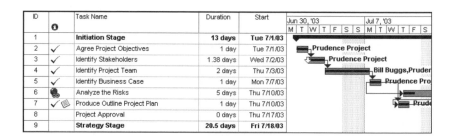

Once you have created a GIF file of the image you want to use, you can include it in an export map. This is done by entering the file name at step 4 on page 200.

Exporting to XML

To learn XML or XHTML, see the relevant titles in this series.

XML stands for Extensible Markup Language and represents a common standard for document exchange that is growing increasingly popular. It has evolved from, and will eventually replace, HTML (there is currently an interim standard defined as XHTML which allows a HTML document to comply with XML standards).

Microsoft Project now allows you to export an entire project in XML format. This means it can subsequently be read by any other application that also uses XML.

1 Select File>Save As from the Menu bar.

2 In the Save as type box, select XML Format (*.xml).

3 In the File Name box, accept the name Project provides or type a new name for the XML file and click Save.

4 If prompted, click Save without a baseline or Save with a baseline, as required.

5 Open your XML file with a text editor (such as Windows Notepad) and see the content:

In the illustration on the right, carriage returns have been inserted to make the information more readable. Note the following:

- *The first two lines define the file type and schema*

- *Remaining lines are each a field with the format: <name>data</name>*

- *All fields with values are exported*

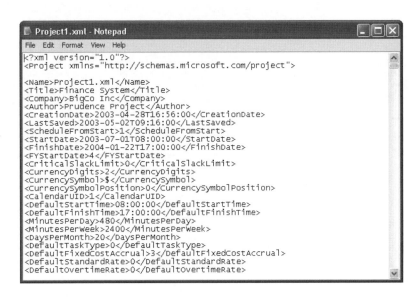

Other File Formats

In addition to exporting information from Microsoft Project in HTML and XML format, you can also export information in Microsoft Excel (workbook or Pivot Table), Microsoft Project Database (MPD), Microsoft Access Database (MDB), Open Database Connectivity (ODBC) compliant, Comma-Separated Value (CSV) or text (TXT) formats.

Exporting to Excel

One of the most useful features is exporting to (and importing from) Microsoft Excel. You can also use Excel graphs and charts to display your project information.

For more information on Excel 2002, see "Excel 2002 in easy steps".

1   Open your project in Gantt Chart view and select View> Toolbars>Analysis from the Menu bar.

2   Select Analyze Timescaled Data in Excel from the new Toolbar and the Export Wizard will open.

3   In Step 1, select tasks 1.1 to 1.7. In Step 2, select Remove Work and add ACWP, BCWP and BCWS. In Step 3, set the dates to a relevant range (see below). In Step 4, select Graph in Excel. In Step 5, click Export.

4   Excel will open and display your data. Select any preferences:

A fairly simple display has been chosen for this illustration. Excel contains many more options for data display.

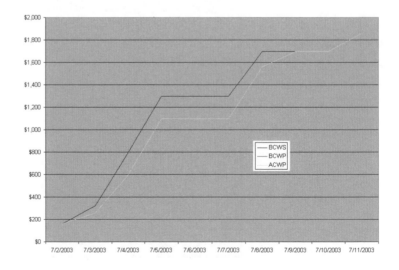

Network Diagrams

This chapter explains what network diagrams (formerly PERT charts) are and how to use them. It shows you how to add nodes, change dependencies and format charts.

Covers

Chapter Seventeen

Network Diagrams

Network diagrams, which used to be known as PERT (Project Evaluation and Review Technique) charts, are also sometimes referred to as activity on-node diagrams. They give you a graphical view of tasks and dependencies. Each task is shown as a box (called a node) which can display up to five fields. The default fields are Task Name, Task ID, Scheduled Duration, Scheduled Start Date and Scheduled Finish Date. The lines linking the tasks reflect the task dependencies.

The shape of each node denotes the level or type of task:

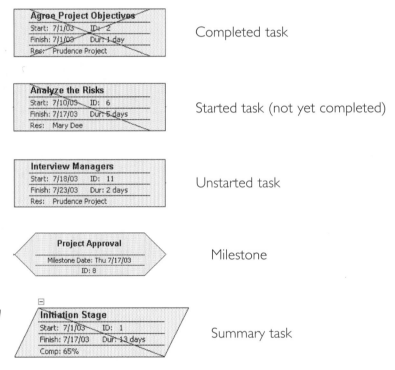

Completed task

Started task (not yet completed)

Unstarted task

Milestone

Summary task

Summary tasks can be expanded or contracted to show or hide subtasks by clicking on the + or − symbols.

Tasks on the Critical Path are shown in red, tasks not on the Critical Path in blue. Filtered tasks are shown in yellow.

The network diagram provides a different type of view of the project from the Gantt Chart but any changes made in either are reflected in the project and the other views.

Network Diagram View

Although Network Diagrams are no longer as popular as they once were (having been largely replaced by the Gantt Chart), they still provide a useful alternative view of a project.

1 Open your project in Gantt Chart view and select Task 6 (Analyze the Risks).

2 Select View>Network Diagram from the Menu bar. The network diagram is displayed with Node 6 (Task 6) selected.

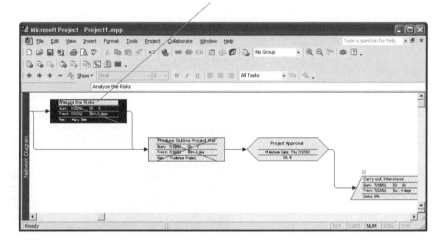

3 Use the Toolbar Zoom In and Zoom Out buttons, together with the scroll bars, to move around the network diagram. Note that you cannot zoom in to more than 400% or out to less than 25%. When zoomed right out, you cannot see any details but if you pause your cursor over a node it enlarges so that you can.

4 Find Task 15 (Consolidate Results), select it by clicking on it and select View>Tracking Gantt from the Menu bar. Note that Task 15 is also selected in the Tracking Gantt. Click on the Go To Selected Task button on the Toolbar to bring the task into view on the Gantt Chart. (Moving between Network Diagram view and Gantt Chart view is very simple.)

Adding a Node

As well as being able to amend task details in Network Diagram view, you can also add a node (task) to the chart.

When you insert a task in Gantt Chart view, it is inserted in front of the selected task. In Network Diagram view, however, a new task is inserted after the selected task.

The F5 key is a shortcut to Go to a Task.

1   Open your project in Network Diagram view and select Node 24 (Agree Requirements) by pressing F5, typing "24" and then pressing Enter. Node 24 is selected and positioned in the view.

2   Position your cursor below Node 24, then drag it to create a box. A new Node 25 is inserted with the Name field selected (the other nodes are renumbered from 26):

Your box will be resized to the same size as the other nodes.

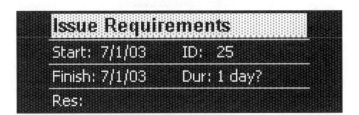

3   Type "Issue Requirements" and press Enter. The duration is automatically set to the default of 1 day. Note that the node is not linked (see the facing page for how to do this).

4   Select Node 28 (Change Budget), click in the Duration field, type "2" and press Enter (this reduces the Change Budget to keep the overall total the same).

5   Save your project file.

As you identify and add tasks (nodes) to the later stages of a project, you should reduce your contingency figure accordingly to keep the overall duration constant.

Changing Dependencies

Once you have added a new node or task you will normally need to make changes to the dependencies to incorporate it.

In Network Diagram view, you select existing dependencies by double-clicking on the linking lines. To create a new dependency, you drag from the preceding task to the dependent task. By default a finish-to-start dependency is created. You can then double-click on the line to make any changes.

If the node you want to connect to is out of view, drag to the left margin and the diagram will scroll.

1 Zoom out and place your cursor on Node 24 (Agree Requirements) and drag down to Node 25 (Issue Requirements). When you release the mouse button the dependency is created and the new node moved into position:

2 Now create a dependency from Node 25 (Issue Requirements) to Node 26 (Select Package). The dependency between Node 24 and Node 26 is now a redundant dependency (as it is implied by the new dependencies you have inserted).

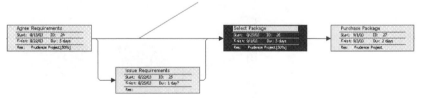

You should note that nodes in Network Diagram view are the same as tasks in Gantt Chart view.

3 Double-click the dependency line between Nodes 24 and 26 and the Task Dependency dialog box opens. Click Delete. The redundant dependency is removed and the nodes realigned:

Filtering

Project 2002 allows you to apply filters in the Network Diagram view. Filtering works the same in this view as in any other. You can use the Filter by box on the Toolbar to select unstarted nodes, nodes allocated to a resource etc.

You can also filter the network diagram to show all successors:

1 Open your project in Network Diagram view, hold down the Shift key and select Node 13 (Produce Draft Requirements). All the successor nodes (14–20) will be selected (brown with yellow lines and white text). Zoom out so they are all in view.

2 Drag the split bar (in the bottom right-hand corner) about halfway up the screen. This will create a split-screen view.

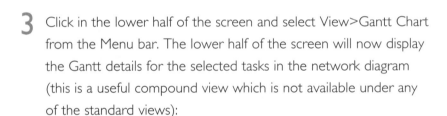

3 Click in the lower half of the screen and select View>Gantt Chart from the Menu bar. The lower half of the screen will now display the Gantt details for the selected tasks in the network diagram (this is a useful compound view which is not available under any of the standard views):

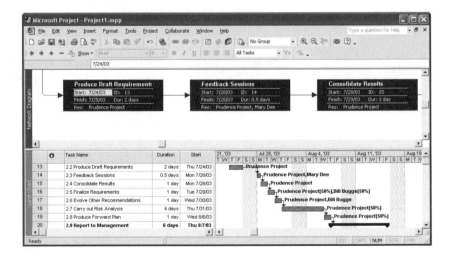

Changing Node Format

Project 2002 gives you control over the number of fields per node, the node shapes and other formatting options. You can specify up to 16 fields per node, change the row heights of cells in the node and change fonts.

"White space" means a chart area with no nodes in it.

1 Open your project in Network Diagram view and ensure you have some white space available.

2 Double-click on a blank area of the chart. The Box Styles dialog box opens:

3 Select the different Style Settings to see a preview of the way they are displayed. Make any changes in the Border or Background sections.

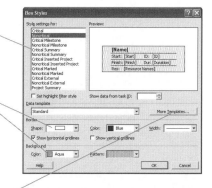

4 Click on More Templates, Summary and then Edit to open the template definition. Click on the next spare cell and select Cost. Click OK, Close and then OK again. Summary nodes now include the cost:

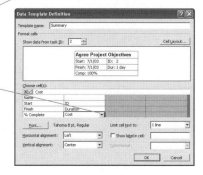

Changing the Layout

Finally you can also change the way that the connecting lines are displayed.

1 Select Format/Layout from the Menu bar. The Layout dialog box opens:

2 Under Link style, select Straight. Select Show page breaks and click OK.

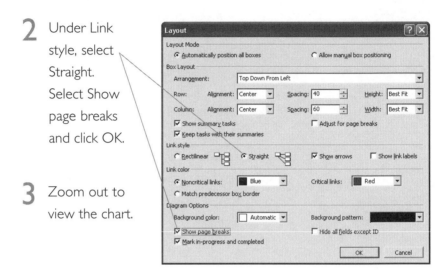

3 Zoom out to view the chart.

4 The connectors are now displayed as straight lines and the dotted lines (indicating the page breaks) are now shown:

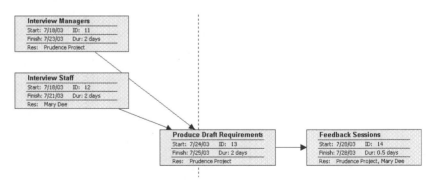

5 Make any further changes you require (or change the link style back to Rectilinear and remove page breaks, if you prefer) and save your project file.

Assigning Resources

You can also deal with assigning resources to a task in Network Diagram view in one of two ways. You can allocate a field in the node box to resource name or resource initials and then type it directly into the field. Alternatively, you can use the Task Information dialog box.

Although we created a new Node 25 (Issue Requirements) in an earlier topic, we have not yet assigned a resource to it.

1 Press F5, type "25" and press Enter to select Node 25 (Issue Requirements) and bring it into view on the chart.

2 Double-click on the node and the Task Information dialog box opens. Select the Resources tab and click in the Resource name field. Click the down arrow, select your project manager and click OK.

3 Switch back to Gantt Chart view and adjust the timescale to bring the relevant task into view. The task has correctly been assigned to your project manager:

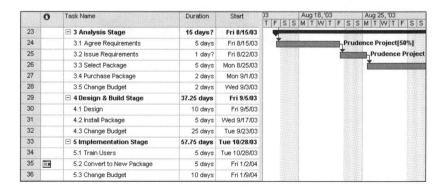

Descriptive Network Diagram

In addition to the basic Network Diagram view there is also a Descriptive Network Diagram view. This shows more details of the selected node.

By combining the Network Diagram and Descriptive Network Diagram views you can get more details of the selected nodes.

1 Open your project in Network Diagram view and select Task 13 (Produce Draft Requirements).

2 Move your cursor to the bottom right-hand corner of the screen so that it changes into the split bar symbol: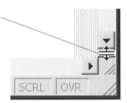

3 Double-click while the split bar symbol is displayed. The screen splits and the Task Form view is displayed in the lower half.

4 Click in the lower pane to make it active. Select View/More Views/Descriptive Network Diagram and click Apply.

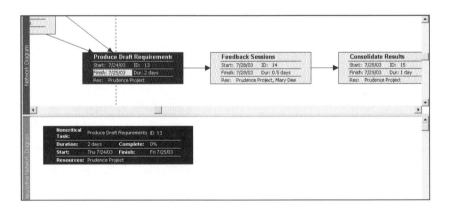

5 Click on different nodes in the top pane and the details are displayed in the lower pane.

Consolidation

This chapter shows you how to consolidate projects, share resources, deal with inter-project dependencies and use workspaces to open multiple projects.

Covers

Chapter Eighteen

Consolidating Projects

If you are responsible for more than one related project, you can create a single, consolidated project file to contain/control them:

1 Open your project file.

You can remove the automatic link if you need to keep the files independent.

2 Now create a new project (Project 2) and set the start date to September 1.

3 Create 4 tasks of 20 days' duration (as below), link them and save the project (but don't close it).

	❶	Task Name	Duration	Start	Qtr 3, 2003 Jul Aug Sep	Qtr 4, 2003 Oct Nov Dec
1		Task 1	20 days	Mon 9/1/03		
2		Task 2	20 days	Mon 9/29/03		
3		Task 3	20 days	Mon 10/27/03		
4		Task 4	20 days	Mon 11/24/03		

To select multiple projects, hold down Ctrl while you click on each project file.

4 Select Window>New Window. Select both projects in the dialog and click OK. The consolidated view of the two projects is displayed in a new file.

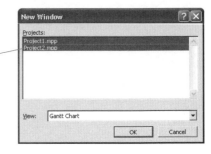

You can add additional projects using Insert> Project from the Menu bar.

	❶	Task Name	Duration	Start	3 Jun	Qtr 3, 2003 Jul Aug Sep	Qtr 4, 2003 Oct Nov Dec	Qtr 1, 2004 Jan Feb Mar
1		⊟ **Finance System**	**143.5 days?**	**Tue 7/1/03**				
1		⊞ **Initiation Stage**	**13 days**	**Tue 7/1/03**				
9		⊞ **Strategy Stage**	**20.5 days**	**Fri 7/18/03**				
23		⊞ **Analysis Stage**	**15 days?**	**Fri 8/15/03**				
29		⊞ **Design & Build Stage**	**37.25 days**	**Fri 9/5/03**				
33		⊞ **Implementation Sta**	**57.75 days**	**Tue 10/28/03**				
2		⊟ **Project2**	**80 days**	**Mon 9/1/03**				
1		Task 1	20 days	Mon 9/1/03				
2		Task 2	20 days	Mon 9/29/03				
3		Task 3	20 days	Mon 10/27/03				
4		Task 4	20 days	Mon 11/24/03				

5 Save the consolidated project file as "Consolidate" and select Yes to save changes to Project 2 and your original project.

Resource Pools

If you are going to have resources working on several projects, you don't want to have to maintain the same resources in more than one place.

Project 2002 allows you to use a resource pool so that you can coordinate the use of the shared resources.

You can set up a new project file to hold your resource pool. Alternatively, you can designate an existing project as holding the resource pool.

1 Open your original project in Resource Sheet view. The resources are all listed. Don't close the project.

2 Open your new "Project 2" in Resource Sheet view. There are no resources in the project.

3 Select Tools>Resource Sharing>Share Resources.

4 Select Use resources, click the down arrow and select your project from the list. Leave "Pool takes precedence" selected and click OK. The resource list from the pool (your original project) is now displayed in the Resource Sheet for Project 2.

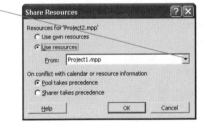

5 Switch back to your original Project and select Tools> Resource Sharing>Share Resources from the Menu bar. The Share Resources dialog box opens displaying the sharing link to Project 2. Click OK.

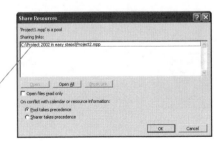

When you reopen your original project, it will ask whether you want to give write access to other projects, restrict access to the original project or create a separate master resource pool file.

Resolving Over-Allocations

Once you have set up a resource pool and begun sharing resources between several projects, you will need to deal with resource overallocations. Fortunately, it is very similar to dealing with resource overallocations in a single project.

1 Open your Consolidate project file. The Open Resource Pool dialog box opens:

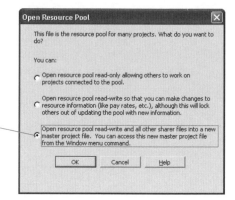

2 Select the third option and click OK. The project file opens together with the linked projects.

3 In Gantt Chart view select Tools>Level Resources from the Menu bar, select Manual calculation and click OK.

4 Select Project 2, Task 1 and assign it to your project manager. Switch to Resource Usage view. There is an overallocation on the project manager.

5 In Gantt Chart view select Tools>Level Resources again but this time select Automatic calculation and click OK. Project 2, Task 1 has been scheduled in and later tasks slipped back on your original project:

When you save the consolidated project file, select Yes to save the sub-project files as well (to keep them in step).

	❶	Task Name	Duration	Start
23		⊟ **Analysis Stage**	**37.75 days?**	**Fri 8/15/03**
24		Agree Requiremen	5 days	Fri 8/15/03
25		Issue Requirement	1 day?	Mon 9/1/03
26		Select Package	5 days	Tue 9/2/03
27		Purchase Package	2 days	Thu 10/2/03
28		Change Budget	2 days	Mon 10/6/03
29		⊞ **Design & Build Stage**	**40 days**	**Wed 10/8/03**
33		⊞ **Implementation Sta**	**32.25 days**	**Thu 12/4/03**
2	📄	⊟ **Project2**	**77.5 days**	**Mon 9/8/03**
1		Task 1	20 days	Mon 9/8/03
2		Task 2	20 days	Thu 10/2/03
3		Task 3	20 days	Thu 10/30/03
4		Task 4	20 days	Fri 11/28/03

Inter-Project Dependencies

As well as consolidating projects and sharing resources, you might have inter-project dependencies. This is where a task in one project is dependent on a task in another project. Dependencies between tasks in different projects can have all the usual dependency types and lag and lead time.

Project 2002 deals with this by creating new pseudo-tasks in each of the linked projects that represent the link.

1 Open the consolidated project file and expand the Analysis stage of your original project.

Note that you can also change the start date through the Task Information box.

2 Position your cursor over the Gantt Chart bar for Task 24 (Agree Requirements). The cursor changes to a four-headed arrow symbol.

3 Now drag from Task 24 down to Project 2, Task 1 and release the mouse button. A link is established.

4 Now create a link from Project 2, Task 1 to the task following Task 24 in the original project. Then remove the redundant link between Task 24 and Task 26.

5 Click the Save button then Yes to All to save the sub-projects.

6 Now switch to (or open) your original project. Notice that Task 1 (from Project 2) has been inserted and is shown in light gray indicating an external task:

If you position your cursor over the external task, the details will be displayed. If you double-click on the Task Name you will switch to the task in Project 2.

	Task Name	Duration	Start	ug '03 4	11	18	25	Sep '03 1	8	15	22	29	Oct '03 6	13	20	27
23	⊟ **3 Analysis Stage**	**37.75 days?**	**Fri 8/15/03**													
24	3.1 Agree Requirements	5 days	Fri 8/15/03		Prudence Project[50%]											
25	3.2 Task 1	20 days	Mon 9/1/03													
26	3.3 Issue Requirements	1 day?	Wed 9/24/03							Prudence Proje						
27	3.4 Select Package	5 days	Thu 9/25/03							Prudence Pr						
28	3.5 Purchase Package	2 days	Thu 10/2/03							Prudence						
29	3.6 Change Budget	2 days	Mon 10/6/03							Prudence						
30	⊞ **4 Design & Build Stage**	**40 days**	**Wed 10/8/03**													
34	⊞ **5 Implementation Stage**	**32.25 days**	**Thu 12/4/03**													

Workspaces

As an alternative to consolidating multiple projects, you may just wish to work with several projects at the same time without consolidating them. If so, you can save them as a workspace. When you open a workspace file, Project opens all the relevant files at the same time.

1   Create two new project files (Project 3 and Project 4) and close all other project files.

2   Select File>Save Workspace from the Menu bar.

3   Name your workspace file and click Save.

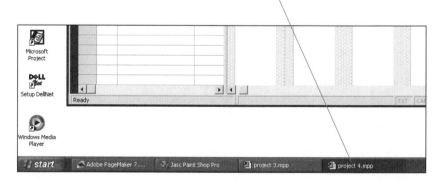

4   Close the workspace and all open projects.

5   Now open your workspace file (*workspace.mpw* in the above example). Project 3 and Project 4 are opened and you can now switch between projects using the appropriate file button on the Windows Taskbar.

Advanced Topics

In this chapter, we take a look at Earned Value Analysis, customizing the Gantt Chart and Toolbars and collaborating with the project team by allocating work and requesting status reports. Then we look at templates and finally some of the additional features available with Project Server and Project Professional.

Covers

Chapter Nineteen

Earned Value Analysis

Earned Value Analysis is a way of measuring project progress in terms of the cost of production.

At the planning stage, the total cost of producing each product (deliverable), and therefore the project in total, is produced. This will typically consist of the resource costs plus any other fixed costs (materials, equipment, fees etc.) which may be incurred. In Earned Value terms, this cost is treated as the value (or worth) of the product/project.

Earned Value has no connection with the benefits of a project, just the costs.

As each product or deliverable is produced (or part-completed, if you wish to measure work in progress), the actual cost of producing it will be known from the time and cost data that you have input for the project.

Using the budget and actual cost, the following three variables are produced:

Budgeted Cost of Work Scheduled (BCWS)
This is the budgeted cost of the work planned to be done in the time being measured. This is the baselined, planned expenditure.

Budgeted Cost of Work Performed (BCWP)
This is the budgeted cost of the work that has actually been completed in the time being measured. It is sometimes referred to as the Earned Value as it is what *should* have cost us to produce the work we have actually completed.

Actual Cost of Work Performed (ACWP)
This is what it has actually cost to perform the work we have completed.

Using the above three figures, a number of calculations can be performed to measure progress in cost terms, such as:

In Earned Value terms, any calculation that gives a negative result is bad!

Schedule Variance (SV)
SV = BCWP–BCWS (how much we should have spent to produce what we have, minus planned expenditure).

Cost Variance (CV)
CV = BCWP–ACWP (how much we should have spent, minus what we have actually spent).

Project 2002 has an Earned Value Report and an Earned Value Resource Table. You can also export Earned Value data to a spreadsheet such as Excel to produce much more sophisticated charts and graphs.

1 Open your project in Gantt Chart view, display all tasks for the first two stages, then select Project>Project Information from the Menu bar. In the Project Information dialog box set the Status date to the date you have input actual data to (7/10/03).

2 Select View>Reports>Costs>Earned Value Report. The Earned Value Report is produced:

Earned Value as of Fri 5/2/03
Finance System

ID	Task Name	BCWS	BCWP	ACWP	SV	CV
2	Agree Project Objectives	$160.00	$160.00	$160.00	$0.00	$0.00
3	Identify Stakeholders	$160.00	$160.00	$160.00	$0.00	$0.00
4	Identify Project Team	$960.00	$960.00	$960.00	$0.00	$0.00
5	Identify Business Case	$400.00	$400.00	$400.00	$0.00	$0.00
6	Analyze the Risks	$27.00	$4.53	$10.50	($22.47)	($5.97)
7	Produce Outline Project Plan	$160.00	$160.00	$160.00	$0.00	$0.00
8	Project Approval	$0.00	$0.00	$0.00	$0.00	$0.00
11	Interview Managers	$0.00	$0.00	$0.00	$0.00	$0.00
12	Interview Staff	$0.00	$0.00	$0.00	$0.00	$0.00
13	Produce Draft Requirements	$0.00	$0.00	$0.00	$0.00	$0.00
14	Feedback Sessions	$0.00	$0.00	$0.00	$0.00	$0.00
15	Consolidate Results	$0.00	$0.00	$0.00	$0.00	$0.00
16	Finalize Requirements	$0.00	$0.00	$0.00	$0.00	$0.00
17	Evolve Other Recommendations	$0.00	$0.00	$0.00	$0.00	$0.00
18	Carry out Risk Analysis	$0.00	$0.00	$0.00	$0.00	$0.00
19	Produce Forward Plan	$0.00	$0.00	$0.00	$0.00	$0.00
21	Prepare Report	$0.00	$0.00	$0.00	$0.00	$0.00
22	Present to Management	$0.00	$0.00	$0.00	$0.00	$0.00
		$1,867.00	$1,844.53	$1,850.50	($22.47)	($5.97)

3 To use the Earned Value Table, switch to Resource Usage view, select View>Table>More Tables>Earned Value from the Menu bar and click Apply.

EAC is Estimate at Completion, BAC is Budget at Completion and VAC is Variance at Completion.

Resource Name	BCWS	BCWP	ACWP	SV	CV	EAC	BAC	VAC
⊟ Prudence Project	$960.00	$960.00	$960.00	$0.00	$0.00	$18,440.00	$14,872.00	$0.00
Agree Project Objectives	$160.00	$160.00	$160.00	$0.00	$0.00	$160.00	$160.00	$0.00
Identify Stakeholders	$160.00	$160.00	$160.00	$0.00	$0.00	$160.00	$160.00	$0.00
Identify Project Team	$320.00	$320.00	$320.00	$0.00	$0.00	$320.00	$320.00	$0.00
Identify Business Case	$160.00	$160.00	$160.00	$0.00	$0.00	$160.00	$160.00	$0.00
Produce Outline Project Plan	$160.00	$160.00	$160.00	$0.00	$0.00	$160.00	$160.00	$0.00
Interview Managers	$0.00	$0.00	$0.00	$0.00	$0.00	$320.00	$320.00	$0.00
Produce Draft Requirements	$0.00	$0.00	$0.00	$0.00	$0.00	$320.00	$320.00	$0.00
Feedback Sessions	$0.00	$0.00	$0.00	$0.00	$0.00	$80.00	$80.00	$0.00
Consolidate Results	$0.00	$0.00	$0.00	$0.00	$0.00	$160.00	$160.00	$0.00
Finalize Requirements	$0.00	$0.00	$0.00	$0.00	$0.00	$80.00	$80.00	$0.00
Evolve Other Recommendations	$0.00	$0.00	$0.00	$0.00	$0.00	$160.00	$160.00	$0.00
Carry out Risk Analysis	$0.00	$0.00	$0.00	$0.00	$0.00	$320.00	$320.00	$0.00

Customizing the Gantt Chart

You can customize a number of things on the Gantt Chart (and indeed on other views) to make it look the way you want. The color and style of the various elements that appear on the schedule can be changed, along with the text font (if applicable).

1 Open your project in Gantt Chart view and Show All Sub-Tasks. Note the summary tasks are all displayed in bold.

2 Select the Task ID field of Task 1 (Initiation Stage) and click the Bold button on the Toolbar to turn it off. The text is now displayed as normal text. Select the other summary tasks and turn bold off.

You can select multiple items by holding down Ctrl as you click them.

3 Select Format>Bar Styles from the Menu bar. The Bar Styles dialog box opens. Scroll down to External Tasks (currently a gray solid bar), select it and change the pattern and color of the middle bar to lines and olive. Click OK and external Task 25 (Task 1 from Project 2) is now displayed in the new style.

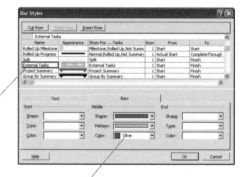

4 Select View>Toolbars>Drawing to open the Drawing Toolbar and click the Text Box button.

5 Drag to create a box to the left of Task 25, type "Project 2 Involvement for Project Manager" and click outside the box.

Custom Toolbars

Toolbar buttons provide quick access to frequently used menu items. In Project 2002 you can create your own custom toolbars, to put all the buttons you often use in one place. You can also create your own buttons for new items. Toolbars are saved in the global template: once you've created a new toolbar, you can use it in any new projects.

1 Select View>Toolbars>Customize from the Menu bar. The Customize dialog box opens. Select the Toolbars tab (there are also tabs for the commands and display options).

After Step 2, the new toolbar isn't much to look at yet but we will add buttons to it in later steps.

2 Click New, type "Custom Toolbar" as the name and click OK. The new toolbar is added to the list and a blank toolbar appears that looks like this:

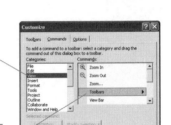

3 Drag the new toolbar away from the Customize dialog box, click the Commands tab and select the View category. The View buttons and commands are displayed. Drag Toolbars from Commands and drop it on your custom toolbar.

4 Now drag Reports to the custom toolbar, then click the Project category and add Project Information. Click Close on the Customize dialog box. Your new buttons are all active.

You can add any buttons or commands to your toolbar and organize it exactly how you want it using customization.

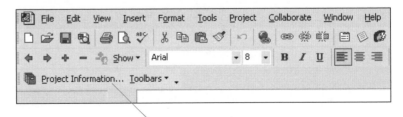

5 Drag your new toolbar below the existing toolbars.

Collaboration

If you have an email system, you can set up collaboration in Project which will allow you to keep in touch with your team by email.

For an email collaboration to be set up, the project manager and the rest of the project team must have:

1. A connection to a network or the Internet.

2. MAPI-compliant 32-bit email.

The project manager must have Project 2002 installed on his/her computer but it is not necessary for the other members of the project team.

Configure for Email Collaboration

If you want this to apply to all new projects, click Set as Default.

1 Select Tools>Options, select the Collaborate tab and select E-mail as the Collaboration option.

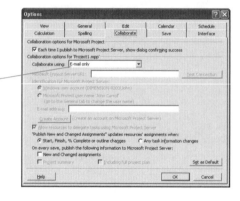

2 Select the General tab and type your name in the User name box. Click OK.

You can also get the Resource Information dialog box by double-clicking on the resource name.

3 To add email addresses for team members select View> Resource Sheet.

4 Select a resource name and click the Resource Information button on the toolbar. Select the General tab, type in their email address and click OK. Repeat Step 4 for each member of the project team.

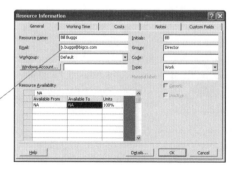

Allocating Assignments

Once the project team is set up, the project manager can assign tasks and request status updates from the project team members. The team members can respond and send notes.

To find out what a button does, pause your cursor over the button to display an explanatory message.

1 Open your project and select View>Toolbars>Collaborate from the Menu bar to open the Collaboration toolbar:

2 Select Task 21 (Prepare Report), click the Publish New and Changed Assignments (second) button, and click OK to proceed. Select Selected Items. Click Edit message text and add the word "please" to the second sentence. Click OK to send the message.

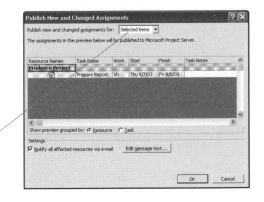

The message will be sent using your default email software and you will be notified of progress and warned of any security issues. An email symbol (envelope) is added in the Information field for the task.

3 Pause your cursor over the Information field to display the relevant status message:

20		⊟ 2.9 Report to Management	6 days	Thu 8/7/03
21	✉	2.9.1 Prepare Report	1.5 days	Thu 8/7/03
22		There has not yet been a response to all the Publish Assignments messages for this new task.	0.5 days	Fri 8/15/03
23			37.75 days?	Fri 8/15/03
24		3.1 Agree Requirements	5 days	Fri 8/15/03

Status Reporting

As well as being able to allocate assignments to the project team, you can also request and submit status reports by email.

Requesting a Status Report

1 Open your project and in Project Information change the status date to 7/18/03.

2 Select Task 6 (Analyze the Risks) and Task 7 (Produce Outline Project Plan).

3 Click the Request Progress Information button on the Collaboration toolbar and click OK to proceed. The Request Progress Information dialog appears with the selected tasks and assigned resources:

4 Make any changes required to the message, enter the required dates and click OK. The message is sent and the Information field on both tasks is updated with an email (envelope) symbol.

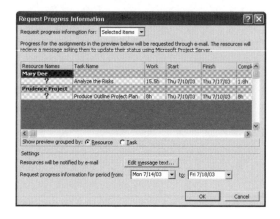

Submitting a Status Report

1 On receipt of the Team Status Request message, enter the actual work performed for the period, the estimated work remaining for the task and any comments.

2 Type any required message in the Message box and click Send. Your status report is submitted.

Templates

Project 2002 allows you to base a project on a template and provides a number of standard templates for you to use. You can also create custom templates.

You may need to insert your Installation CD if the required templates were not originally installed.

I Close any open project files and select File>
New. Select General
Templates
then the Project
Templates tab.

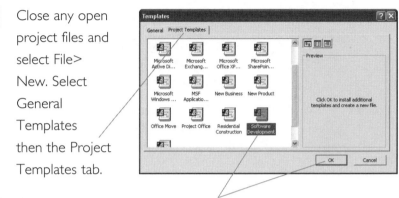

2 Select the project template you wish to use and click OK. The Project Information dialog box opens for the start date etc. and the file is created based on the template.

Creating Custom Templates

It is equally straightforward to create your own custom templates from an existing project file:

You can find where your template files are by selecting Tools>Options> Save from the Menu bar.

I Open your project in Gantt Chart view and select File>Save As from the Menu bar. The Save As dialog box opens.

2 Select Save as type: Template and select the directory where your Project 2002 templates are stored (typically *C:\Documents and Settings\Name\Application Data\Microsoft\Templates*) and click Save. The Save As Template dialog box opens.

Also, you will probably need to clear any constraints.

3 Select the checkboxes for any of the data you want to be cleared from the template (baseline values, actual values, etc.) and click Save. You can now create a new project based on this template.

Project Server

Although it is possible to share project information by email, the introduction of Project Server 2002 provides a much more sophisticated method for sharing project information. It can be accessed directly from Project 2002 but it can also be accessed using a Web browser such as Microsoft Internet Explorer.

Access from Project 2002

The Collaboration toolbar (and Collaboration menu) give access to the Project Server functions:

The Publish functions (all information, new and changed assignments, project plan and republish assignments) all make use of Project Server once Collaboration has been set to use it.

1 Select Tools> Options. Select the Collaborate tab:

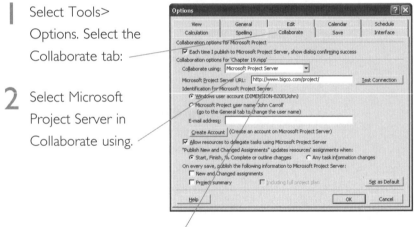

2 Select Microsoft Project Server in Collaborate using.

3 Enter the URL of the server and click OK.

4 Now the Collaborate functions will all use Project Server in place of email:

5 In addition to Publish and Request functions, Project Center, Documents and Issues (the three right hand buttons) will all now activate Project Server functions.

Web Access

With Project Server Client Access Licenses (CALs), project team members can access Project Server without needing to have Microsoft Project as long as they have a suitable Web browser such as Internet Explorer.

Microsoft Project Web Access is consistent with the other Microsoft Office Web applications (such as Outlook Web Access). Each team member is allocated a home page which displays their current, role-specific details. These would include any newly assigned tasks and action items. They can also save views with sorting, grouping and filtering options making it easy to review pertinent information on a regular basis.

Project Center

Using Project Center from Project 2002, you can get an overview of all the projects that you are involved in on Project Server. You can drill down into the project information, group projects using outline codes, filter and search. Project Center views can also be customized with graphic indicators and you can receive alerts if a project is behind schedule or over-budget.

Timesheets

The Timesheet view provides a flexible method for team members to report progress on their tasks. As the project manager, you can choose the tracking method that best suits each project (hours worked or percentage of work completed). When the timesheet is updated through Web Access, the changes are displayed in red for easy visibility.

To-Do Lists

Users can create and manage to-do lists online in the same format as a task list. It can be converted into a full project plan if necessary.

Documents and Issues

Documents can be linked to projects and shared with other users.

Issues can be entered by any team member and the issues can be associated with individual tasks or with projects. You can then assign ownership, track progress and record resolution.

Project Professional

Project Professional is aimed at the enterprise and must be used in conjunction with Project Server. It contains the same functionality as Project Standard but it also provides a number of additional features aimed at the enterprise:

Enterprise Resources

Resource assignments throughout the enterprise are accessible to all project managers, resource managers and other authorized project stakeholders. This provides accurate enterprise-wide resource availability and for amendment the resources can be checked out, edited and checked back in again.

Project Professional also contains a Resource Substitution Wizard which analyses the skills needed by a project (including generic resources) and matches them with the skills available throughout the enterprise and determines availability.

It also allows the project manager to find resources throughout the enterprise with the required skills and availability using filter and query. Resource availability graphs also use enterprise data to show where resources are under- or over-utilized.

Resource Center provides all these additional features.

Enterprise Customization

Project Professional supports global enterprise templates with tailored fields, calendars, views, modules and any other Project elements. This allows a consistent approach across the enterprise. Individual project templates are also available through the enterprise database.

Enterprise-wide custom fields with formulae, outlines and pick lists can also be defined again to give a standard approach to the project management processes.

Portfolio Analyzer gives authorized stakeholders access to real-time project and resource information across the enterprise. It allows them to interact with the data through Pivot Tables and charts.

Portfolio Modeler can be used to model what-if scenarios and experiment with different versions of the same plan by interactively modifying project schedules and resources.

Index

D

E

F

G

H

I

J

K

L

M

S

T